Authority Control in the Online Environment: Considerations and Practices

Authority Control in the Online Environment: Considerations and Practices

Barbara B. Tillett
Editor

The Haworth Press
New York • London

Authority Control in the Online Environment: Considerations and Practices has also been published as *Cataloging & Classification Quarterly*, Volume 9, Number 3 1989.

The Haworth Press, Inc., 12 West 32 Street, New York, NY 10001
EUROSPAN/Haworth, 3 Henrietta Street, London WC2E 8LU England

Library of Congress Cataloging-in-Publication Data

Authority control in the online environment : considerations and practices / Barbara B. Tillett, editor.
    p. cm.
    "Has also been published as Cataloging & classification quarterly, volume 9, number 3, 1989" – T.p. verso.
    Includes bibliographical references.
    ISBN 0-86656-871-9
    1. Authority files (Cataloging) – Data processing. 2. Catalogs, On-line. I. Tillett, Barbara B.
Z693.3.A88A86 1989
025.3'22 – dc 19   88-30649
                                                                                CIP

Authority Control in the Online Environment: Considerations and Practices

CONTENTS

ABOUT THE EDITOR

Barbara B. Tillett, PhD, MLS, is Head of the Catalog Department at the University of California, San Diego. She held previous positions as Director for Technical Services at the Scripps Institution of Oceanography Library as well as Science and Technology Reference Librarian/Bibliographer and Director of the Ocean Science Information Center at the Hamilton Library, University of Hawaii.

Founder and former Chair of the Authority Control Interest Group within the American Library Association (ALA LITA/RTSD Interest Group on Authority Control in the Online Environment). Dr. Tillett now serves on the RTSD CCS Policy and Research Committee and on the CCS Executive Committee. An active member of LITA, she planned the authority control technical session and workshop for the 1988 LITA Conference in Boston.

Considerations for Authority Control in the Online Environment

Barbara B. Tillett

This collection on authority control is intended to offer background and inspiration for future thinking. In the next pages you will find considerations in sharing authority records nationally and internationally, perspectives on recent research and theoretical studies, results of some new research with suggestions for future research, descriptions of the design of three different computerized authority control systems along with the impact of two such systems on library operations. The focus is on name and title authority control with only passing mention of subject authority control because subject authorities have received a great deal of attention in recent literature.

The topic of authority control recurs whenever cataloging rules are reviewed or whenever new forms of catalogs are introduced. In the past ten years since the LITA Authority Control Institutes revitalized interest in authority control, there has been considerable useful research on authority control. Many computerized authority control systems have come and gone, while some have persisted and grown. There is still much to be done to develop the "perfect" computerized authority control system and file design for online catalogs.

Authority control for a library catalog can be viewed from two different perspectives depending on whether the catalog "user" is a library patron or a cataloger. Each perspective has different functions. For the library patron, authority control collocates related names, titles, and subjects and helps the user match his or her own

Barbara B. Tillett, PhD, is Head of the Catalog Department, Central University Library, University of California, San Diego, La Jolla, CA 92093-0175.

search terms with those controlled access points used in the catalog. For the cataloger, authority control provides unique, consistent headings (i.e., access points) with appropriate references for variations in form and links to related headings in accordance with a given set of cataloging rules and rule interpretations. As you will see in Taylor's literature review of research on authority control, the past five years in particular have brought valuable insights regarding the nature of headings and references in library catalogs and the difficulties with shared authority files. But why do we have authority control?

At the turn of the century Charles Cutter identified two basic functions of a library catalog: finding function and gathering function. The finding function enables a user to determine if a library contains a particular item specified by its author or title. The gathering function, also known as collocation, enables a user to determine (1) all the works of a particular author that are held in a library (gathering them together under the name of the author), (2) which manifestations of a work (e.g., editions) are in the library (gathering them together under a uniform title), and (3) what items the library has on a given subject (gathering them together under a specific subject heading). The following article by Smiraglia indicates the importance of authority control's syndetic devices to link related works and manifestations of works. In order to accomplish the finding and gathering functions, the catalog must have authority control. Authority control is inherent to a catalog and without it, a file cannot be considered a catalog.

In the environment of shared cataloging and union catalogs, authority control becomes essential in order to avoid duplicated records and to match records contributed from various sources. For union catalogs, whether in printed form or microform, it is useful for the contributing libraries to share the same authority file *or* to have a single authority file control the headings used in the union catalog with the ability to recognize and match incoming variations. For the most part, computers cannot recognize matches unless they are programmed to make the match or are given text to use in making a one-to-one comparison. Likewise for links between headings—the computer must be programmed with information about what links exist or how to determine the linking relationships between headings. The computer cannot match a heading coming in on a machine-readable tape to a heading in the union catalog or online catalog, unless it has been told how to make that match or has been given all the expected variations that are to be considered a match.

The term "authority control" is probably one of the most misused terms in recent library literature and especially in vendor brochures. This is due to the fact that the processes that are to be included in authority control via computer are evolving. In particular, authority control and authority work are *not* the same, but have often been mistakenly interchanged.

Authority work includes the research work and intellectual effort involved in creating and updating authority records. The Library of Congress has created authority records at least since 1889 as indicated in its Rules on cards. To insure that the works of a personal author or corporate body are brought together when an inquiry is made, the cataloger must determine whether the name has been used before, and if so, in what form, so that it may be consistently applied to the new bibliographic record. If the name to be used for a heading is not found, the cataloger must establish the form to be used for a heading, following agreed-upon conventions, such as the *Anglo-American Cataloguing Rules*, 2nd edition, and the Library of Congress's rule interpretations. The extra work of tracking down variant forms of the name and relationships to other names must also be done, since the cataloging rules do not always produce the heading a library user would ask for . . . as we all well know!

Authority work also includes recording the authority data of preferred form, variants, history, scope, and links to other authority records. The result is an authority record often recorded on a card in an authority file. We now have a MARC format for communication of machine-readable authority records, so our files can be shared online. The various MARC formats have been one step in the success of the Name Authority Cooperative Project (NACO and now the NCCP) and the Linked Systems Project (LSP) through standard formats for sharing bibliographic and authority records.

Authority work also involves the maintenance of authority files and the corresponding maintenance of associated bibliographic records and references in the library's catalog.

The *authority file* then is a set of authority records. Headings within an authority file are usually consistent and unique within that file.

Authority control is the overall term for the concept encompassing the operations of authority work and emphasizing the control over variant forms of access points. According to Arlene Taylor, authority control is "the process of maintaining consistency in headings in a bibliographic file through reference to an authority file."[1]

Dr. Taylor defines *automated authority control* as "the use of a computer to manage large portions of the process of authority control."[2] I prefer to think of it as the computer's role in authority work, plus a more general control over the access points and search terms used in the computerized bibliographic file, for example, the computer-assisted establishment of authorized headings, including automatic validation and automatic verification of headings entering a catalog. Automated authority control could also include the matching algorithms, including normalizations of capitalization, spacing, punctuation, and diacritical marks, for a system that is a bit more forgiving of the typed in search terms a user tries or a cataloger enters. We now consider these as separate computer functions, but since they are intended to control the search terms and access points in the computer, they could be considered authority control. Additionally, the computer systems that automatically provide for permutations, truncations, keyword search or approximation, soundex algorithms, and stemming from root words of the access points during the search or matching process could be considered part of authority control. Maintenance capabilities for insuring consistency of headings, such as global changes, are also considered part of authority control in the computer environment. The key here is control of access points and search terms.

Perhaps the term "access point control" is less confusing than authority control to describe the control of headings. I think it is important to use a term that gets away from the connotations of "authority," because our notion of a single authoritative form changes when we utilize headings in local catalogs. We currently have cataloging rules that focus on the needs of the individual library. Cataloging rules give preference to the predominant form found in the library's collection. That predominance will vary from library to library. Even within a given library predominance may change as more works are acquired. Furthermore, we may wish to include several forms of name found in various authoritative sources and to indicate a default, that is a preferred display form for a heading or access point, based on the online system's determination of which form is predominant, or we may wish to allow the user to select a form they prefer as they view the online catalog. The user's choice might be preferable for a user preparing a bibliography from the results of a search of the online catalog. The main point is to link the variant forms of names and related names to provide collocation and pathways through the catalog's resources rather than to dictate authoritative form. In the past it has been most convenient to attach the links and variations to the form authorized by the cataloging rules, but the computer may offer new possibilities.

Name variations are diverse. The article by Fuller refers to the variations she has discovered in items controlled through library catalogs and provides us with important data on the need for authority records in the online environment. It may be useful for the development of computer systems that link name variations to identify the categories of name relationships. As a by-product of my dissertation on bibliographic relationships, I developed a suggested taxonomy for name relationships and offer it here for future study (see Appendix).

Also related to preparations for my dissertation, I did a literature survey in 1982 of authority files and authority control. At that time I had 361 citations starting with the famous debates in the mid-1800s over Panizzi's cataloging rules, in which he argued in favor of a catalog as opposed to a finding list (that is, the need for authority control in a sense). My literature survey now has over 450 items with the majority written in the last 8 years. Interest surged in the late 1970s with the change to AACR2. Libraries were seeking ways for machines to help change headings to conform to the new cataloging rules. Global change was in the air. And now there is a renewed interest in authority control as we see more and more libraries installing online catalogs.

However, most of us still have card catalogs and rely on the

Library of Congress for bibliographic and authority records. Some of us are relying on national bibliographic utilities, such as OCLC, RLIN, WLN, and UTLAS for bibliographic and authority data, which they send us on computer tapes, on computer output microfiche, or catalog cards—depending on the utility and our requests. All of these bibliographic utilities offer online access to the Library of Congress Name Authority File, also known as the LCNAF, and the Library of Congress Subject Headings, LCSH. The article in this collection by Dickson and Zadner evaluates the use of LCNAF on the RLIN system. RLIN and UTLAS have authority files from their members as well as LC's files, for example RLIN has the New York Public Library's authority file, which is used by some of its members. WLN allows for individual authority files, but typically its members utilize the LC authority file. WLN was the first bibliographic utility to have an authority file and preceded MARC formats for authority records, but now has changed to the MARC format. OCLC has the least flexibility for its members. It offers LCNAF and LCSH for online searching, but has not yet worked out a procedure to allow individual libraries to identify that they have used an authority record, nor can they have the authority record read onto their archival tape or have cards produced for the cross references for their catalogs. However, a few libraries with local automated cataloging systems are able to download authority records from OCLC into their local files. Still others print cards through PC applications using OCLC's authority records.

Some vendors and book jobbers that offer cataloging services also provide authority files or say they have authority control, and the source of authority data varies, although most do follow LC's authority. When considering a system that claims to provide authority control, be sure to ask what that means to the vendor, what the source of the authority file is, and how often it is updated.

There have been arguments over the necessity for authority control in the online environment for over 10 years. But as Henriette Avram noted at a 1983 ALA meeting of the heads of technical services of large research libraries, based on present-day evidence, authority control *is* necessary, and it is now time to get on with how to best provide for authority control at the least cost.

As you are probably aware, studies of costs of authority work have been conducted over the past few years. R. Bruce Miller, now Assistant University Librarian for Technical Services at the University of California, San Diego and formerly at Indiana University and the University of Texas at Austin, did a study of costs of authority work, on which he reported in 1979, showing that academic libraries in combination spend millions of dollars each year on authority work that is often redundant. In some libraries nearly half or over half of the cost of cataloging is attributed to authority work. If the authority work were shared, the costs could be considerably reduced, just as we have done with shared bibliographic records through the bibliographic utilities. The NACO Project is an effort to do just that, share the effort of establishing authoritative headings and their references. Started in 1977 by the Library of Congress, NACO, the Name Authority Cooperative Project, was boosted by funds from the Council on Library Resources and has made great progress. The related Linked Systems Project (LSP) furthers the ability to share authority work by providing online links with telecommunications protocols to allow different computer systems to connect and work with each other. The result of these projects is, of course, a national resource authority file, online, that can be shared by libraries everywhere and maintained by the NACO participants. There are now over 60 NACO participating libraries.

So one important part of reducing overall costs for authority control for the nation's libraries is the availability of a national or perhaps even a future international resource authority file. Delsey's article in this collection indicates the difficulties in creating and maintaining an international resource authority file. But despite these difficulties, national files do exist, and the master records in the national authority file are then available to catalogers in individual libraries. The authority records can be downloaded and modified as needed for local use.

If we have a local computerized system, whether an online catalog, an automated circulation system, or some other computerized processing system, the bibliographic records that we have shared at the national level are loaded on to our local system for local use. In the 1984 authority control opinion poll conducted for the LITA/RTSD CCS Interest Group on Authority Control in the Online Environment, many respondents suggested a distinction between the needs for the national resource authority file versus the needs for a local authority file, where the national resource authority would preserve the decisions made by national libraries and the local authority file would reflect the needs of local users and the capabilities of the local system.[3] The influence of the national authority decisions are apparent in the shared records we load on our local systems. In order to maintain authority control, we take on LC's or some other authority practices, sometimes with slight local variations. When LC changes an authoritative heading, we usually try to change our authoritative heading to match LC. A major drawback to this workflow is that we do not yet have a good mechanism for knowing which headings LC has changed. There is no alerting system, and we only find out about the change when we have a new bibliographic item that has the changed heading or when we discover the change while maintaining another heading or cross reference.

Among the world's libraries there is more to be cataloged than can be done by any one library. Some of what is to be cataloged is ephemeral or of minimal use. The Library of Congress has been following "minimal level cataloging" for several years for those materials it has identified as low use. Minimal level cataloging forgoes most of the access points normally provided in cataloging and reduces the amount of normal authority work. That is, the personal and corporate names used as main entry and as the first added entry in a minimal level record are checked against the existing catalog, and if found, the authorized heading is used, but if not found, LC sets up the name according to AACR2, but without references for variant forms and without determining relationships to other names. This sort of minimal level authority work, which omits references, may be an efficient approach, since you will see in Fuller's article in this collection that most headings do not require cross references. For those headings that do need cross references, the minimal level approach causes more work for the catalog user, who will probably need to try alternative access points when the name is not found. However, minimal level authority work is a good, practical solution to speed up processing for materials expecting little use, recognizing that future online upgrading can be done to the national authority records to add references and links. It should be recognized that even now there is constant change to authority records for names established by the Library of Congress and the NACO participants. A maintenance system and upgrading features are extremely important not only for minimal authority work and cataloging but for full cataloging and authority work as well.

Another way to reduce the costs of authority work is to utilize computers to do post-cataloging authority work. That is, let the computer verify incoming headings against its authority file and tell the cataloger of any non-matching headings. The online system might also be able to automatically flip incoming headings that match a reference, but probably only after human review to avoid inadvertent mismatches. The following articles by Kirby, Goldman and Smith, Ridgeway, and Gibbs and Bisom provide views of three systems in operation today.

Where do we go from here? We have a good beginning for sharing the creation of authority records, and we have the start of a mechanism for shared maintenance, albeit limited to NACO participants. Computers are providing us with capabilities for matching user's terms with the controlled terms used in cataloging, for reducing some authority work, such as global update of forms of headings, and for national level sharing of authority data, primarily Library of Congress-based. Computer capabilities will continue to develop and formats for authority control records will continue to evolve. What remains constant is the continued need for control of names and works to provide access from their variant forms and to indicate related names and works. This need may be met in new and different ways with future technologies. I hope this collection of papers will provide you with inspiration for meeting those future challenges.

NOTES

1. Arlene G. Taylor. "Authority Files in Online Catalogs: an Investigation of Their Value," *Cataloging & Classification Quarterly* 4, no. 3 (Spring 1984): 2.

2. *Ibid.*

3. Barbara B. Tillett. "1984 Automated Authority Control Opinion Poll: a Preliminary Analysis," *Information Technology and Libraries* 4, no. 2 (June 1985): 177.

APPENDIX

A list of name relationship terms was compiled during my review of cataloging rules for bibliographic relationships. From that list the following taxonomy suggested itself and is offered here for future study.

SUGGESTED TAXONOMY FOR NAME RELATIONSHIPS

I. Variations of a given name
   A. Equivalence relationships
      1. Orthographic relationships
         a. Spelling variations
         b. Transliterations
         c. Translations
         d. Punctuation variations
         e. Capitalization variations
      2. Word order relationships
         a. Inversions
         b. Permutations
      3. Fullness relationships
         a. Full name
         b. Abbreviation
         c. Initialism
         d. Acronym
   B. Alternative names
      1. Synonyms
         a. Pseudonym
         b. Byname
         c. Names with titles
         d. Official name (for a position)
         e. Religious name
         f. Changed name
            1) Persons
            2) Corporate bodies
            3) Conferences
            4) Geographic places
         g. Title variations of items
            1) Cover title

    2) Spine title
    3) Caption title
    4) Binding title
    5) Running title
    6) Uniform title
    7) Parallel title
    8) Distinctive title
    9) Added title page title
    10) Half-title page title
    11) Other title
    12) Key title
    13) Augmented titles
    14) Variant access title
    15) Cataloger's title
    16) Series traced differently

II. Related names
  A. Shared name/title
  B. Hierarchies
    1. Family hierarchy
    2. Corporate hierarchy
    3. Jurisdictional hierarchy
    4. Title hierarchy
  C. Genealogy
    1. Family genealogy
    2. Corporate genealogy
    3. Geographic place name genealogy (evolution)
    4. Title genealogies (evolution)

    [Note: When the evolution of the name of a person is involved, the relationship is equivalence or alternative name]
  D. Geographic proximity relationships

Authority Control
in an International Context

Tom Delsey

SUMMARY. This paper traces the efforts made by IFLA (the International Federation of Library Associations and Institutions) over the past three decades to promote the concept of Universal Bibliographic Control in relation to authorities and authority control. It covers the work done by various groups within IFLA to develop standards for personal and corporate name headings, for authority and reference entries, and for UNIMARC/Authorities. The paper concludes with a summary of possible models for the future development of a systems infrastructure for international authority control.

Although terms such as "authority control" and "authority system" have come into use only relatively recently, it is clear that the ideas lying behind such terms have been with us for a much longer time. The concept of authority control, though not stated in those terms, is implicit in virtually all the statements of principle relating to the objectives of the catalogue enunciated in the past century and a half. What we have seen in that time is the progressive development of the idea from the abstract to the concrete. It should not surprise us to find, therefore, that the idea of authority control at the international level, though seemingly quite new, has also emerged from a concept of much longer standing. To understand the objectives and rationale for an international authority system, one must

Tom Delsey is Director, Acquisitions and Bibliographic Services Branch, National Library of Canada. Within IFLA he has served as chairman of the Working Group on an International Authority System; as a member of the Steering Group for a UNIMARC Authorities Format; and is currently chairman of the Standing Committee of the Section on Cataloguing.

look first to its antecedents in the concept of Universal Biblio-graphic Control (UBC).

For most of us the UBC concept is best known through its embodiment in various IFLA programs and publications related to bibliographic description: the ISBDs, the *Guidelines for the National Bibliographic Agency and the National Bibliography*, and the UNIMARC format.[1] The framework within which those particular programs function rests on two fairly straightforward principles: first, that each country should assume responsibility for the bibliographic control of its own publications; and second, that the records produced by each national bibliographic agency should be made available to be used by all other countries for the cataloguing of those same publications. Perhaps less well known are the parallel principles embedded in the UBC concept that relate to authorities: that each country should assume responsibility for establishing authoritative headings for its own personal and corporate authors; and that the authority records produced by each national bibliographic agency should be made available to be used by all other countries requiring authorities for those same authors.[2]

Whether one applies the principles of UBC to bibliographic description or to authorities, the conditions that must be met in order for any implementation of the concept to succeed are the same. First, there must exist a mutually accepted canon of principles, standards, and practices governing the formulation and structure of the cataloguing data. Second, each national bibliographic agency must execute its responsibilities in a manner that is both comprehensive and consistent with the agreed standards. Third, there must exist an infrastructure that supports the efficient exchange of data between and among national bibliographic agencies. In practice, of course, it is unrealistic to expect that all these conditions will be met universally, but the degree to which they are or are not met will either extend or limit the effectiveness of any attempt to implement bibliographic or authority control on an international scale.

The work that has been done within IFLA over the past twenty-five years or so to give substance to the UBC concept as it relates to headings for personal and corporate names and to authorities has been guided largely by a recognition of the need to deal with those three factors critical to successful implementation of the UBC concept: standardization of practices for the establishment of headings and the structuring of authorities; promotion of national responsibilities for the creation and dissemination of authority records; and the planning of an infrastructure to support effective international exchange of authority data.

The earliest work on this front was directed toward standardizing practices with respect to headings for personal and corporate names. The work began, in fact, with IFLA's first major effort to advance the concept of UBC, the formulation of the Paris Principles. Although the agenda for the International Conference on Cataloguing Principles held in Paris in 1961 dealt with a broader range of issues than just the form and structure of personal and corporate headings, the principles governing the establishment of such headings did receive significant attention, and the agreements reached at the conference played an essential role in laying the groundwork for future work in this area.[3] Perhaps the most significant work following on from the Paris conference, in fact, was that done by Eva Verona, under IFLA's sponsorship, to explore in greater detail the complex issues relating to corporate headings and their ramifications in the international world of cataloguing conventions.[4] Verona's work in turn served as the basis for the deliberations undertaken by the Working Group on Corporate Headings and ultimately for the approval and promulgation of the recommendations put forward in IFLA's *Form and Structure of Corporate Headings* in 1980.[5] Follow-up on the Paris conference's agreements with respect to personal name headings took a somewhat different form. In recognition of the inextricable link between national conventions for naming and the cataloguing treatment of personal names, IFLA undertook not to "standardize" the cataloguing conventions in the normal sense, but to codify the various national conventions underlying the naming of persons, and hence to provide a rationalized basis for the formulation of personal name headings along lines of national origin. The results of that effort were published in three successive editions of *Names of Persons* issued in 1963, 1967, and again in 1977.[6]

The concessions made to the primacy of national conventions for the names of persons in the Paris Principles are indicative of a fundamental recognition running throughout the Principles of the strong bond that exists between national traditions of language, culture, and social structures, on the one hand, and the traditions that underlie national cataloguing conventions, on the other. To impose on headings for personal names emanating from a particular national tradition a structure that runs counter to the conventions of that tradition is simply not effective. It is irrelevant whether the imposed structure is one borrowed from another national tradition or one invented expressly for purposes of achieving an international norm, that is, a kind of Esperanto structure. With corporate names we encounter the same phenomenon. The Paris Principles and the recommendations adopted for the *Form and Structure of Corporate Headings* reinforce a respect for the language of origin of corporate names, whether they be the names of corporate bodies, territories, or international institutions. Hence the acceptance of the vernacular as the basis for the authoritative heading, and only in the extreme, a "universal" form such as "Ecclesia catholica."

When viewed from a strictly national perspective the principles of linking catalogue headings to national convention and the vernacular in one sense serves as a perfectly rational basis for achieving the objectives of the catalogue. And, again from the national viewpoint, the approach would work perfectly in practice as long as the only names in the catalogue were those of domestic origin. But that, as we know, is seldom if ever the case. So a problem arises when we juxtapose the contents of the catalogue—which for the most part will encompass names derived from a multiplicity of national and linguistic traditions—with the users of the catalogue—who, again for the most part, will represent a single national and linguistic tradition. In this situation, the same linguistic and cultural traditions that serve to shape the form of catalogue entries for names of national origin have tended to exert their influence on foreign names "imported' into the catalogue as well. As a result, names in the catalogue derived from foreign traditions have in many instances been altered to conform with the dominant linguistic and cultural traditions of the domestic users of the catalogue. The degree of alteration has varied with the type of name. It has tended to be most pervasive with geographic names used in headings for governments and in the various titles, epithets, and qualifiers that form part of both personal and corporate name headings. To some degree the effects of domestic cultural dominance have also been evident in the structures imposed on headings for legal documents, officials of state and the like, where a pattern derived from domestic traditions is imposed upon headings for their counterparts in foreign cultures. From a pragmatic point of view the assimilative approach to the problem that arises from disparities between the contents of the catalogue and the traditions of its users has been reasonably effective. But the solution has been undeniably national in nature, and although the general approach may have been common from one nation to another, the particulars of the linguistic and cultural precedents that have been established and of the alterations made to headings of foreign origin have varied markedly from one nation to another.

When one shifts from the national to the international context, the dimensions of the problem are, of course, greatly increased. But more importantly, in the international context the solution conventionally applied at the national level itself becomes problematic. Under the first principle of UBC each country assumes responsibility for establishing authoritative headings for its national authors. For that purpose the link between the catalogue heading, national conventions, and the vernacular is ideally suited to produce the most appropriate heading. But under the second principle of UBC, all other countries are expected to accept such headings in their authoritative form as established by the country of origin. If this second principle were applied strictly, each country would forego the conventional adaptation of headings of foreign origin to suit the predominant linguistic and cultural traditions of its own catalogue users. To the credit of those who have promulgated the UBC concept and the succession of principles and recommended practices that have evolved from that concept, significant strides have been made in the last twenty years toward practical acceptance of the notion that headings for names of foreign origin should respect the conventions and linguistic forms of their source. The national cataloguing codes that have been developed or revised subsequent to the adoption of the Paris Principles have gone much further than their predecessors in accepting the vernacular as the basis for the form of corporate headings and in respecting national convention in structuring headings for personal names. As these principles have been embedded in national cataloguing codes the catalogues that are produced under those codes have begun to shed much of their national and linguistic bias. And as those catalogues have changed, the process of assimilating headings created by foreign cataloguing agencies has changed. Headings that once would have required adaptation to conform with the domestic bias of the catalogue can now be "imported" directly without modification because the form of name on which they have been based is the same as that accepted as the basis for the heading under national cataloguing rules. To the extent that this compatibility has been achieved, the ground has been cleared for the acceptance of headings established in the country of origin as the universally authoritative form.

Although there was still much work to be done in promoting acceptance of the principles elaborated in *Names of Persons* and those being developed for the *Form and Structure of Corporate Headings*, toward the end of the 1970s the IFLA UBC program began to shift its focus somewhat from the formulation of headings per se to matters pertaining to authority lists and the international exchange of authorities independently of the headings embodied in catalogue entries. With a view to developing the necessary standards and infrastructure to support the exchange of authorities, a survey was undertaken to collect data on the content of authority files currently created by national bibliographic agencies and details on the maintenance and distribution of those files. The results of the survey were compiled in 1978 by the IFLA International Office for UBC.[7] That same year the IFLA Section on Cataloguing and the Section on Mechanization drew up terms of reference for a Working Group on an International Authority System to address a number of tasks related to standardizing the content and structure of authority records, both in print and machine-readable form, and to the development of a "system" for authority control and the exchange of authority data on an international scale.[8]

The agenda that the Working Group set for itself was structured on the premise that the development of an international authority system could only take place through the long-term implementation of successively staged "building blocks," each designed within the context of an overall conceptual framework. In its skeletal outline that conceptual framework envisioned the ultimate form of an international authority system as a network of interrelated national databases of authority records surrounding a central facility that would serve to control traffic in the network in the sense that it would manage the links between related authority records emanating from various national centres and redirect logical "packages" of authority data to the appropriate national centres. As a model this framework is not unlike those that have been adopted at both the local and the national level where the objective has been to capture and reconcile authority data originating from multiple sources and to redistribute a logically integrated file of authority data to participants in the "system." The challenges at the international level, however, were seen to be considerably more complex than would normally be encountered at the local or national level, not only with respect to the ultimate configuration of the system and the interworking of its components, but even at the most rudimentary level of data elements and record structures.

It was clear from the outset that any systematic exchange of authority data, whether it was to be effected through the conventional print media or through more elaborate automated means, would require the establishment of an internationally accepted norm to govern the content and structure of the authority entry. The survey of national authority files conducted in 1978 had revealed a wide range of variation in practice from one country to another. One of the first tasks undertaken by the Working Group was to extrapolate from existing practice a common set of data elements and a uniform structure that would serve to provide a standard for the presentation of an authority entry in printed form. In some ways the task was analogous to that undertaken by IFLA in developing the ISBDs as the standard for the presentation of bibliographic descriptions. There was a difference, however, in that the standard for authority entries would not, for the most part, be required to deal with matters such as the form and structure of the data elements that serve as the constituent parts of the authority entry, for the key data elements had already been addressed through such documents as *Names of Persons* and *Form and Structure of Corporate Headings*, and would ultimately be governed by the particular rules for the formulation of headings embodied in national cataloguing codes. What was required was a standard that would stipulate the elements to be included in an authority entry—headings, references, tracings, notes, etc.—the order in which those elements were to be presented, and a formal system of punctuation to demarcate each of the areas and elements of the entry.

As the work on that standard evolved it became clear that there were in fact three distinct forms of entry to be dealt with: the authority entry itself, the reference entry, and the general explanatory entry. It is only through a combination of all three entry types that an authority list can be compiled so as to clearly reflect the relationships between the established or authoritative form of heading and the variants that might be sought by the user. It was in fact the handling of these relationships, the conventions that would be adopted to reflect them, and the options that might be permitted for combining the authority entry with the reference entry in a single display that proved to be the most challenging aspect of the task before the Working Group. Eventually all the problems were worked through, a completed draft was prepared for worldwide review, final approval was given by the sponsoring Sections within IFLA, and the end product was published in 1984 as *Guidelines for Authority and Reference Entries.*[9]

The *Guidelines*, as they were published, deal explicitly with authorities for personal names, corporate names, and uniform titles for anonymous classics. Within the context of international exchange, those three types of heading were seen to form the core, both in the sense that they would account for the greatest volume of headings and insofar as they would likely have greater exchange value in terms of their use by countries other than the one from which they originate. Nevertheless, the general framework for authority and reference entries embodied in the *Guidelines* was designed with the expectation that it would serve, perhaps with some modification, to accommodate authorities for other types of headings as well. In fact, when the *Guidelines* were completed they were referred to the International Association of Music Libraries and the International Association of Law Libraries with a view to having experts in those two fields develop, as necessary, extensions to the basic framework to accommodate authorities for uniform titles for musical compositions and legal works. The *Guidelines* were also referred to the IFLA Section on Classification and Subject Cataloguing so that experts in that area could determine whether the general framework might be adapted for use with subject authorities.

In establishing a norm for the presentation of authority entries and for the references that accompany them in authority lists, IFLA had taken a significant step forward in its program to promote the international distribution and use of authoritative headings created by national bibliographic agencies. The Paris Principles and the work on personal and corporate headings that had followed their adoption had laid the ground by establishing agreed practices for the formulation of headings and promoting a more receptive climate for the international use of headings established in the country of origin. The *Guidelines for Authority and Reference Entries* provided a more efficient vehicle for the distribution of those headings and their associated references. As authority lists produced by the various national bibliographic agencies begin to incorporate the approved specifications for the content and structure of authority and reference entries they will prove to be more readily usable by other agencies. Adherence to the *Guidelines* should mean that the time-consuming processes of supplementing foreign authorities with additional information and restructuring the entries to conform with the national standard for the entry should be all but totally eliminated. In addition, the prescribed punctuation demarcating the various elements of the entry should serve to clearly identify the functional relationships between elements and thus eliminate ambiguities that might arise because of limited knowledge of the language in which the authority is cast.

The *Guidelines for Authority and Reference Entries* have served another purpose that is equally if not more important for the international authorities program as a whole in that they have provided a base for developing an international format for authorities. In that sense the *Guidelines* are analogous to the ISBDs: they provide a norm for content structure around which the core of an internationally accepted specification for a machine-readable record could be developed. Recognizing that the development of a format for authorities to parallel the UNIMARC format for bibliographic records was key to the realization of even the most basic form of automated authority control on an international scale, IFLA identified that as its priority among the tasks that remained to be dealt with after the Working Group that developed the *Guidelines* had completed its work.

A Steering Group was set up in 1984 to oversee the development of UNIMARC/Authorities. The parameters for the format had already been set. In terms of content it must accommodate all elements defined in the *Guidelines for Authority and Reference Entries*, encoded in such a way as to support their display as specified in the *Guidelines*. On the technical side the format must conform with the general structural characteristics of the UNIMARC bibliographic format, and must be compatible in detail with respect to the fields that are common to both formats, specifically the fields containing headings. UNIMARC/Authorities has now undergone several major revisions in draft, each having been reviewed by the Steering Group, and is currently being distributed worldwide for comment prior to its finalization and publication. Perhaps not surprisingly, the major difficulties encountered in developing UNIMARC/Authorities were similar to those that had challenged the Working Group in developing the *Guidelines*. Foremost among the difficulties were questions of structure. The complexities of the relationships between authority headings, references, and tracings that had been so difficult to deal with in the *Guidelines* resurfaced in UNIMARC/Authorities, but in a somewhat changed context. For printed displays the most straightforward way of dealing with these relationships is through a clean separation for the three entry types: authority entries, reference entries, and general explanatory entries. Even the *Guidelines*, however, could not be so restrictive, and of necessity incorporated a number of options for combining related authority and reference entries in a single display. For UNIMARC/Authorities the challenge was to find the most efficient means of encoding the data required to produce authority and reference entries, and not necessarily to have the boundaries of the machine-readable record coincide with those of the printed display. By its nature a machine-readable record is more flexible than a printed entry, and can be structured in such a way as to support more than one form of display, thus obviating the need for redundancy of data that so often occurs in printed entries. With UNIMARC/Authorities one of the fundamental issues that had to be dealt with is the question of just how far the format should go in accommodating variant approaches to the structuring of the authority and reference data it is designed to convey. The *Guidelines* had shown that options for display of the data had to be allowed. The options that could be incorporated in a machine-readable format were, if anything, even more numerous. The UNIMARC format for bibliographic records gave ample demonstration of the degree of flexibility that could be built into a format for handling relationships similar to those required for authorities, most notably in the alternatives it offered for handling item-series relationships. Experience with the UNIMARC bibliographic format, however, had shown that in practice allowing multiple options for encoding such data, while it might simplify conversion at the source from a national format, tended to complicate conversion for the receiving agency attempting to deal with a multiplicity of what in effect are different implementations of UNIMARC. For that reason there was a conscious effort made to minimize structural options within UNIMARC/Authorities. In many respects that has made the task of developing the format more difficult, but ultimately the effort should yield significant benefits for the users of the format and should help to ensure that data encoded in the format can be processed with equal efficiency regardless of its source.

With the finalization of UNIMARC/Authorities and its implementation by national bibliographic agencies a major milestone in the IFLA program for international authority control will have been reached. At that stage the authorities program will have attained, on a technical level at least, the same plateau as the bibliographic program. Bilateral exchange of authority data on an international basis will be supported by a standard format embodying an entry of standardized content and structure. But when one looks more closely at the complexities of authority control on an international scale, one soon realizes that an infrastructure more sophisticated than that supporting simple bilateral exchange is required.

What we come back to is a recognition of the gap that still remains between the ideal embodied in the UBC concept and the realities of national practice with respect to authorities. The situation that exists today and is likely to persist for the foreseeable future is that despite the gains made in promoting the international acceptance of headings as established in the country of origin, differences in language, script, and conventional usage continue to work against the viability of completely universal acceptance and use of authorities across national boundaries. While the proportion of headings regarded as universally acceptable may be increasing, there are still significant numbers that will vary from one country to another either because of elements within the heading that convention dictates must be adapted to the language of the catalogue user, or because the strength of conventional usage within the country takes precedence over acceptance of a heading in its "original" form. That being the case, any system intended to establish authority control, in the normal sense of the word, at an international level must be designed in such a way as to accommodate linguistic and national variants in the accepted form of heading for any given person, corporate body, or title, while at the same time ensuring that all such variants are interrelated and linked to the single identity that they represent.

In order to implement such a system, whether in a centralized or distributed mode, it is essential to have in place a device that will facilitate the linkage of variant authorities for the same identity, preferably in a form that would lend itself to efficient handling in an automated environment. In its original model for an international authority system, the Working Group envisaged that device as an international standard number, similar to the ISBN and ISSN. The number would serve to identify the object of the authority entry, whether it be a person, a corporate body, a work, or a subject, and would be present in all variant records for that same object as the common element that would link them all regardless of the form of the heading. In an ideal implementation the standard number would be assigned by the national bibliographic agency designated as the agency responsible for establishing the authoritative heading under UBC. The number would also be recorded in conjunction with the heading in any bibliographic record in which the heading might be used. Once the heading and its corresponding number were registered, any other national bibliographic agency adapting the heading for use in its own national authority file would record the standard number with its variant version of the authority. Any subsequent importation either of bibliographic records carrying the heading or of variant authorities emanating from other national bibliographic agencies would trigger an automatic adjustment to conform with the national adaptation, and the records would then be cleanly integrated with the national file.

Although the technical requirements for a device such as a standard number are reasonably straightforward, the practical aspects of administering the assignment of the numbers are far from simple. On the one hand, a decentralized model for administration, where each national bibliographic agency assumes responsibility for assigning numbers to its own national authors, presupposes a clearcut definition of the term national author that could be applied in such a way as to raise no questions about which country should have responsibility for assigning the standard number to a particular individual or corporate body. In practice, of course, there are countless instances where both individuals and corporate bodies elude such neat categorization. And if that is true for our contemporaries, the problem is even more complex when viewed in retrospect, where we must deal not only with the peregrinations of individuals and corporate bodies, but with the shifting of national boundaries as well. If the complexities are ultimately judged to be so extensive as to rule out the possibility of a decentralized, nationally based administration of standard numbers, the only alternative would seem to be a centrally organized administration with international responsibilities for assigning standard numbers. The size and scope of such an operation would in themselves present a significant challenge, not to mention the difficulties of actually reconciling variant authorities as they were submitted by a multiplicity of national agencies to ensure that all related variants were properly registered under the same standard number.

Yet it is difficult to conceive of a system supporting authority control on an international scale without some sort of central facility to serve at least as a gateway for the coordination of activities carried out at the national level. Without a central database to serve as a register of authority entries and their corresponding standard numbers it would be next to impossible for national agencies to establish that vital link between the entries in their own authority files and the standard number that will identify the variant forms of heading that have been used by other agencies and which will be circulating as headings in bibliographic records emanating from perhaps dozens of different national agencies. While much of the processing involved in reconciling variant forms and replacing headings in bibliographic records with the preferred national variant can be handled in a distributed mode at the national level, all such processing would be dependent on the key function of registering standard numbers having been carried out in some sort of centralized fashion. And if a central facility could be put in place to handle the registration function, there are a number of compelling arguments that could be made in support of having that facility perform other functions as well. In the preliminary model developed by the Working Group on an International Authority System, the central facility was seen as performing a kind of clearinghouse function for the redistribution of authority entries that had been adapted to meet the language requirements of a particular catalogue. In the typical scenario outlined by the Working Group, an authority entry originating in France might be exported to the USA, where elements of the heading would be modified for compatibility with headings in a national authority file geared to English language users. If there were a central clearinghouse facility, the modified entry could be routed to that facility, and from there be redistributed to all national agencies that had identified themselves as sharing the same profile with respect to language and cataloguing code. In this particular example, the potential recipients of the modified entry would include, among others, the British Library, the National Library of Australia, and the National Library of Canada, the latter of which would likely have also accepted the original entry from France for use in its unmodified form as the French language entry in its bilingual authority file. What one would expect to achieve by implementing a clearinghouse model of this sort would be an optimization of the basic principle of economy that underlies the UBC concept. Short of achieving the ideal where a single authority entry gains universal acceptance in its original form, the clearinghouse model ensures as far as possible that changes necessitated by linguistic differences are made only once for each language, and are then shared by all agencies having the same language requirement.

To date, most of the thought given to models such as those outlined above for the administration of standard numbers, and for the registration and clearinghouse functions have been largely speculative. Some preliminary analysis of requirements was carried out by the Working Group on an International Authority System, but that was done primarily for the purpose of sketching out the context within which the basic "building blocks," the standard authority entry and the machine-readable format for authorities might eventually be expected to function. An enormous amount of work remains to be done not only on the technical aspects of an international authority system, but on the administrative complexities and the cost-benefits of various schemes for its implementation. It is likely to be the non-technical issues, in fact, that ultimately determine the extent to which the concept of Universal Bibliographic Control is realized as an international system for authority control.

NOTES

1. The current editions of the International Standard Bibliographic Descriptions (ISBDs) include *ISBD(G): General*, 1977; *ISBD(M): Monographic Publications*, 1987; *ISBD(S): Serials*, 1987; *ISBD(NBM): Non-book Materials*, 1987; *ISBD(CM): Cartographic Materials*, 1987; *ISBD(A): Antiquarian*, 1980; and *ISBD(PM): Printed Music*, 1980. All are published by the IFLA UBCIM Programme, British Library Bibliographic Services, London. *Guidelines for the National Bibliographic Agency and the National Bibliography* (Paris: Unesco, 1979). *UNIMARC Manual* (London: IFLA UBCIM Programme, British Library Bibliographic Services, 1987).

2. Dorothy Anderson, *Universal Bibliographic Control: A Long Term Policy* (Pullach/Munchen: Verlag Dokumentation, 1974) p.47.

3. For details, see International Conference on Cataloguing Principles, Paris, 9th-18th October 1961, *Report* (London: Clive Bingley, 1963) pp. 51-59; 81-86.

4. Eva Verona, *Corporate Headings: Their Use in Library Catalogues and National Bibliographies* (London: IFLA Committee on Cataloguing, 1975).

5. International Federation of Library Associations and Institutions, *Form and Structure of Corporate Headings* (London: IFLA International Office for UBC, 1980).

6. For the most recent edition, see International Federation of Library Associations and Institutions, *Names of Persons: National Usages for Entry in Catalogues*, 3rd ed. (London; IFLA International Office for UBC, 1977). A supplement to the third edition was published in 1980.

7. IFLA International Office for UBC, "Survey of Authority Files and Au-

thority Control Systems for Catalogue Headings: First Report,'' mimeographed (London, 1978).

8. For details on the terms of reference and recommended tasks, see *International Cataloguing* 9 (1980): pp. 10-12.

9. International Federation of Library Associations and Institutions, *Guidelines for Authority and Reference Entries* (London: IFLA International Programme for UBC, 1984).

Research and Theoretical Considerations in Authority Control

Arlene G. Taylor

SUMMARY. Research and recent "theoretical" discussions of authority control are synthesized and organized into the following groups: general overviews; need for research; need for unique access points for names; need for authority control outside traditional library catalogs; reference structure for names and its relationship to users' needs; authority control for works; authority control for subjects; need for authority files; and, technological considerations. Conclusions are drawn about the need for research in the area of file design.

Two reviews of authority control literature were written in 1982—one published and one not. In the published review Auld summarized authority control as presented in the literature of the preceding 80 years.[1] In a very thorough seminar paper, Tillett included citations to 411 works, all but 13 published after 1960.[2] One might wonder, then, if it already could be time for another review. Read on! So much has been written on the subject in recent years that it has been necessary to limit the scope of this review. In his review Auld observed:

> The literature dealing with automated authority control can be categorized into two primary groups: the practical and the philosophical. The practical is dominated by description of file structures, programs for working with these files, and both

Arlene G. Taylor, PhD, is Associate Professor, School of Library Service, 609 Butler Library, Columbia University, New York, NY 10027.

real and envisioned products. . . . The theoretical papers, a
minority, examine the function of authority control for the future.[3]

The incidence of "philosophical" or "theoretical" literature has
since increased, including a number of papers that report the results
of research. I have chosen to include in this review research conducted in the area of authority control and also some of the papers
published in the 1980s that deal with "philosophical" aspects, although they present no empirical data. "Practical" articles (using
Auld's definition) are, for the most part, omitted. In addition the
work of Auld and Tillett is not repeated here. Rather, this review
draws relevant background from those reviews in the process of
organizing, synthesizing, and drawing conclusions from the more
recent work on the various aspects of authority control covered
here.

GENERAL OVERVIEWS

Three authors were mentioned by Auld as having made especially useful contributions to the theoretical understanding of authority control. These were Schmierer, Runkle, and Malinconico.
Schmierer discussed the practical and theoretical need for authority
control.[4] In the process she identified how the "finding" and
"gathering" functions of the catalog both require authority control.
Runkle discussed the different authority control procedures needed
in the online environment—especially in a shared online database
where records from several institutions should mesh.[5] In the article
cited by Auld, Malinconico provided a carefully structured justification of the need for authority control.[6] In another article from that
same time period, Malinconico looked at the future advances that
technology would allow.[7]

Several recent articles have discussed the topic from a philosophical point of view. In 1983 Henderson identified future expectations
for authority control as including: automatic maintenance of logical
structure of the authority file itself, including indication of relationships between headings; linkage of authority and bibliographic
files, with authority headings and references serving as indexes to

bibliographic records, and with changes in authority files being automatically reflected in bibliographic files; control of hierarchical levels of corporate names and subject headings; validation of newly input records (i.e., using *authority control* as a form of *quality control*); compatibility of multiple bibliographic files; and increased sharing of the work involved in building authority files.[8]

Avram in 1984 made the argument that, while authority control is admittedly costly, there are economic advantages to its being performed at the highest level of the networking hierarchy so that there is less duplication of effort.[9] However, it was also clear to Avram that for large databases that have not had authority control, the cost of imposing it would be very great. She recommended that the cost benefits of different degrees of authority control at different network levels should be investigated. There seems to be some confusion here and in several other articles between use of the terms "authority control" and "authority files." Authority *files* can be provided for reference at the highest level, and even authority *control* can be provided for the database at that level, but unless the local library uses that database as its catalog, there will have to be continuing authority *control* (with the resultant need to maintain authority *files*) at the level at which the database for the catalog is held, in order to handle ongoing changes in terminology, names, etc.

In a textbook approach in 1985 Clack summarized the topic with definitions, purposes, and brief discussions of the issues, posed as questions.[10] She had also published a bibliography on authority control in 1983.[11]

In 1986 Runkle asserted that authority control had been enhanced in many libraries because they had followed Library of Congress (LC) cataloging practices closely.[12] He suggested that further enhancement would occur if LC's card catalog were converted to MARC format, because "its authority structure could serve as the base against which other retrospective conversion is performed."[13] He speculated that lack of interest by research libraries in such a conversion resulted from LC's lack of interest, combined with a fear of competition by vendors and bibliographic utilities, and a negative attitude toward LC because of resentment that LC's cataloging is assumed to be better than anyone else's. Runkle believed that libraries actually have followed LC standards, not because it is necessarily "the best," but for consistency, for their authority system, and because they do more cataloging than anyone else. Thus, it is efficient to follow LC, and it serves scholars by providing "cross-catalog consistency."[14]

Interestingly, Oddy made exactly the same point about libraries in Great Britain using cataloging from the British Library Bibliographic Services (BLBS):[15]

> The success of NAL [BLBS' *Name Authority List*] stresses a growing trend: that libraries in this country are prepared to accept centrally produced headings in the same way in which American libraries accept those produced by Library of Congress—not so much for the quality (whatever that means in this context) as for their consistency and the network of authority records which accompany them. . . . There's a cost benefit to libraries in following BLBS practice, but there's also a benefit to users in the consistency they then find between catalogues.[16]

An intriguing suggestion from Oddy is that the next version of AACR might be addressed to authority control:

> . . . we could envisage an AACR part one concentrating as now on rules for producing standard bibliographic descriptions, and a part two giving instructions on how to link these to existing authority records, and how to create new authority records. This would be a true cataloguing code for machine systems.[17]

NEED FOR RESEARCH

Until the 1980s there had been very little research in this area, but there had been numerous calls for such research. In her review Tillett mentioned several such calls.[18] Richmond's suggestions for research possibilities for the online catalog in 1976 included three problems related to authority control.[19] Butler asked in 1979 for more information about what the user really wants.[20] Miller in 1979 and Koel in 1981 asked for more cost studies. Miller had found that the University of Texas at Austin had spent $1.25 per title on name/title authority control, amounting to $145,000 for the 1977/78 fiscal year. He calculated that the ARL libraries spent about $5 million in 1979 dollars for authority control per year. He then noted, "we do not even know empirically if rigorous authority control is actually necessary."[21] Koel reported that authority work at Yale took 5-10 times as much time as description of a work.[22] Mosey, whose 1980 thesis was one of the first pieces of research on authority control, suggested several areas for further research, as is the custom when reporting results of serious research.[23] We now, of course, have many examples of such suggestions in the reports of research discussed in the following sections.

In 1981 Svenonius, calling for research in all areas of cataloging, commented:

> . . . questions of efficient file design need researching, such as how is linkage information to be accessed, should all linkage information be contained in an authority file, and how are authority and bibliographic files to be interfaced? But again, it is necessary to stand back. The fundamental question here is how much authority control is really needed. It may be argued . . . that linking related items . . . is not cost-effective. This argument is already being tested in the market place; a more rational approach would be to test it by research.[24]

NEED FOR UNIQUE ACCESS POINTS FOR NAMES

One of the earliest examples that used research to illustrate the need for authority control was in a 1969 article by Lubetzky and Hayes.[25] The point of the article actually was to justify the need for unique identification of *works* in a bibliographic environment, but in the process, the authors graphically illustrated the need for authority control of names. A few entries for persons surnamed "Gibbs" were chosen from the 1966 cumulation of *Science Cita-*

tion Index. These were researched for adequate identification. One person listed as "Gibbs" was also listed as "Gibbs J H." Another listed as "Gibbs" was also listed as "Gibbs J W." "Gibbs C J" was actually "Gibbs C V," and so on.

Wiggins set out in 1984 to determine whether there was support in the literature for the need for unique access points.[26] He found no empirical research on the subject, saying,

> The conclusion drawn from this literature search is that [the importance of unique access points] is indeed an area that warrants further study and research, from the vantage point of both the user and of those who manage systems that are already in place. This is especially true because virtually none of the items cited is actually based on empirical research. Studies in this area could help validate the importance — or unimportance — of unique access points.[27]

Wiggins found several articles that suggested that the uniqueness of the access point does not matter very much if terms and names are cross-indexed and there is a reference structure that will ensure that the user retrieves what is relevant in the system. Two authors in particular were noted in this regard. Malinconico had written in 1980 that new systems would be able to handle intricate indexing of various forms of the same access points in different records, thus rendering uniqueness of individual headings unimportant.[28] The next year Williamson, predicting the nature of catalogs in 2006, made reference to invisible linkages of variant forms of names to retrieve all items of a particular person or entity.[29]

Auld's review noted the same concept as having been articulated by Gorman in 1978. He summarized Gorman's prediction as saying that "the presence of authority control will be transparent or invisible to the user. Any form of a heading entered by the user will lead directly to the appropriate bibliographic record without intermediary steps being required of the user."[30]

Tillett pointed out in her review that,

> In 1969 Lubetzky described online catalogs as providing "correlation" by indicating all the various forms of an author's

name, so that a query under any one will produce a listing of all works published under different names. . . . He notes that this ability removes the problem of choice of name by which an author is to be identified in the catalog.[31]

Tillett went on to show that a means for accomplishing this "correlation of names" had already been suggested by IFLA in 1980 in its recommended establishment of an international standard authority number (ISAN). She noted also that in 1975 Poncet had advocated such a number, which he felt would allow for local display of the preferred variant for a name; and that in 1979 Malinconico had proposed a similar approach.[32]

Without citing any of the aforementioned works on the future lack of need for unique access points, Burger in 1984 stated that authority work is about to "shift from choosing a proper heading, with applicable cross-references, to identifying only the various manifestations of a name. . . . "[33] He posited this conclusion as both a result of the presence of artificial intelligence (AI) in online cataloging systems and a justification for future applications for AI.

While this approach has appeal in liberating us from the necessity for choosing one form of name as the "correct" one, we must also remember that catalog users, who may not understand our concept of authority control, may be confused by being given bibliographic records that seem to have no obvious relationship to the name they entered. Hildreth, in 1982, noted this concern, showing an example of a search request for personal author "David St. John" that yielded a list of eight short one-line citations.[34] The first five began with "Hunt, Howard, 1918-," the next two with "St. John, David, 1949-," and the last with "Wright, Charles, 1935-." There was no explanation that Howard Hunt has used the pseudonym "David St. John." (The last item was written about "David St. John," and presumably contained some of his work.) If we abandon choosing one form as the "correct" one, our systems need to be sophisticated enough to present the user with authority records first in instances where more than one name or form of name has been used by one person or body, so that in the above example the user could have a chance to observe all the names used by one such author and to choose which "David St. John" was the one wanted. There should also be the option of displaying titles related to one such person grouped separately from titles related to another.

Some recent research has attempted to discover how much scattering of names there would be in a catalog if variant forms of name were not brought together in some way. Shore reported in 1984 a study that sampled personal names from the online "authority file" of the Regenstein Library, University of Chicago.[35] This file was actually a file consisting of every unique heading used in the bibliographic file, and therefore, the file contained more than one entry for some names (e.g., those that had been used as subjects as well as authors, and those that represented authors of works that had had uniform titles created for them). Because famous people and prolific authors thus had a greater chance of being drawn in the sample, the results had to be weighted, which perhaps was one of the important results of Shore's study: it dramatized the need for careful sampling from bibliographic and authority files. The purpose of the study was to determine the proportion of names that appeared in one form in the catalog heading, but in another form on chief sources of information for the name in question. She found that 59 percent of the title page forms were the same as the heading, and 64 percent were the same if one looked only at the nonprolific authors (defined as having fewer than 10 items in the catalog). However, the rules used for forms of headings ranged from the 1908 Anglo-American code to AACR 2, and the study did not measure the variation in use of name by each particular author.

In an attempt to deal with some of the limitations Shore had encountered, Fuller conducted a study in 1986 to learn the proportion of occurrences of variation in name usage by individual authors.[36] Fuller was careful to attempt to overcome the sampling problem experienced by Shore. Her methodology should be read by anyone who wishes to sample from a bibliographic file. She found that about 16 percent of the sample authors used names in variant forms. Her work is being published elsewhere in this issue.

No research comparable to that of Shore and Fuller has been found for corporate names or for other types of headings, although work in progress by the author under a grant from OCLC is addressing variation in corporate names, as well as continuing study of variation in personal names.

NEED FOR AUTHORITY CONTROL OUTSIDE TRADITIONAL LIBRARY CATALOGS

Several authors have written about the need for authority control in settings other than the traditional library catalog. In 1983 Elias and Fair looked at the need for authority control in an electronic office system.[37] They demonstrated the retrieval problems that developed after three people stored data entries involving corporate names for six months. No name authority control system had originally been created; thus, the same person would index the same entry in several different ways, e.g., "Wall Street Journal," "Wall St. Jnl.," "WSJ." In Elias's master's paper, upon which the Elias/Fair article was based, Elias found that 37.4 percent of the corporate names entered into the system appeared in at least two different forms.[38] In an attempt to solve the problem, a list of names was generated and one form chosen as the authoritative one. However, the persons creating the entries were under too much time pressure to consult the list. The solution was to create a set of "rules" for constructing the names. The patterns were easy to learn, and the system thus was improved. Elias and Fair suggested that librarians' skills with authority control are sorely needed wherever databases are being created.

A series of articles have appeared that address the problem of searching for names in the many online databases that are now available. Pasterczyk discussed in 1985 the complications that multiple transliteration schemes for the Cyrillic alphabet add to the variations that already exist within and among databases.[39] She delineated a series of strategies to use in searching variant spellings, variant initials for forenames, letters transliterated as apostrophes, and translated names. She also gave tips for searching through particular systems: SDC, BRS, and DIALOG. In essence, this article is a mini-lesson in performing authority work, except that it is up to the user, not the cataloger, to do the work every time a search is performed.

Piternick, in 1985, wrote in general terms about use of names and titles to find information on topics rather than on the person or work named, e.g., "Lou Gehrig's Disease."[40] She recommended that when names represent concepts, indexers should include them as identifiers, and compilers of thesauri and controlled vocabularies should include them as entry terms.

Pilachowski and Everett (and Everett and Pilachowski) wrote three articles in 1985 and 1986 on searching for names in online databases — one each in the areas of social sciences, current events, and humanities.[41,42,43] Their discussions were limited to searching names as subjects. They identified particular databases in each discipline and then gave specific suggestions for the best ways to search for names as subjects in each database. In a similar article in 1986, Snow discussed strategies for finding names for people in medicine.[44] She included searching for authors as well as for names as subjects, and she emphasized generic search strategies rather than specific databases.

One is struck, while reading this series of articles, by the immense complications that can sabotage the unwary (or even the initiated). Is it possible for a searcher to be able to remember all the tricks necessary for a complete name search? One wonders why more effort is not made in commercial databases to perform authority control at the indexing level (as is done in a few databases, e.g., the Author Index Manufacturing System [AIMS] for *Chemical Abstracts Service*, but is relatively rare) rather than requiring it of the users. It has to be suspected that money is at issue. Not only would it cost the for-profit enterprises a great deal to provide name authority control, it would cut users' online search time. Pasterczyk pointed out, "No matter which search service is used, a complete author search will take much more time than a quick-and-dirty one."[45] Libraries, for the most part, are not-for-profit agencies, and thus have different priorities.

Another advocate of a nontraditional application of authority control was Evans, an archivist, who wrote in 1986 that the traditional method of providing access to archival holdings, the "record group" concept, should be replaced by the concept of authority control.[46] The record group concept assumes that records come from agencies that exist in mono-hierarchies and that those hierarchies do not change, split, reorganize, etc. Evans stated: "Applying the record group concept to finding aids produces static, out-of-date inventories that provide access to records only through a single, hierarchical path."[47] He asserted that disadvantages of this system can be

overcome by changing to a system "in which records and the rec-
ord-creating agencies exist in a multi-dimensional conceptual
space,"[48] a concept embodied in the concept of authority control.
Evans' article should be read by every librarian for its insights into
how concepts and theories of bibliographic control that have developed in libraries over the period of many years can be used in other
contexts to assist in the processes of records management wherever
they exist.

REFERENCE STRUCTURE FOR NAMES
AND ITS RELATIONSHIP TO USERS' NEEDS

As technology progressed and more libraries invested in online
catalogs, researchers began to investigate whether the reference
structure developed through the years for manual catalogs would
suffice for online catalogs. In 1984 Taylor reported findings from a
study of online catalog users' name searches that had resulted in no
"hits" in the NOTIS online catalog of Northwestern University.[49]
Northwestern's NOTIS at that time did not have keyword searching, and in order to find names it was necessary to input the search
in the exact order it would be entered in a card catalog. Taylor
identified 35.8 percent of the searches as "bound to fail" (e.g.,
obvious typographical errors, use of the wrong file command,
forename input before surname). The remainder were searched in
Northwestern University's NOTIS, OCLC, RLIN, and/or MUMS
(LC) in order to determine whether such a name existed, and if so,
whether linked authority records would have provided references
that would have led the user to records for the name sought. She
found that only 6.4 percent of the "zero hit" searches would have
produced "hits" had the authority file been linked to the bibliographic file. In contrast, 40.1 percent of the searches would have
produced "hits" if the system had been programmed: (a) to "flip"
names to search last name first, and (b) to search the first word of
the user's input string followed by the first letter of the second word
(e.g., to place the user in a browsable index near the sought-for
name input by the user).

One of Taylor's findings was that 22.1 percent of the "zero hit"
searches resulted because the user used a variant spelling of a part

of a name.[50] Only about one-fifth of these would have been retrieved using one of the system programs she had suggested. However, there are programs that could have assisted in these cases. In 1985 Roughton and Tyckoson wrote about two sound-based codes, the SOUNDEX code, used since the 1930s to search for names in census files, and the Davidson Consonant Code, used since the early 1960s to search for misspelled names in airline passenger reservation systems.[51] Both codes have other successful uses. The authors described the codes and delineated uses for them in authority files and online catalogs. They suggested that such codes could be integral parts of authority records.

Thomas reported in 1984 a study to determine whether references necessary for authority control in a manual system would also be necessary when searching MELVYL, the automated system to which she had access.[52] A sample of references for corporate and personal name headings was selected from the local AACR 2 authority file on cards. These included both references authorized by LC and references added locally for original cataloging or to enhance LC records. Each reference was examined to determine whether it was appropriate/necessary in MELVYL's online keyword search environment where right-hand truncation of searches is automatic. Thomas found that 47 percent of the references would be unnecessary for MELVYL. These consisted primarily of (a) references that were less full in form than the established heading form, and (b) references that consisted of word-order inversions.

Jamieson, Dolan, and Declerck reported in 1986 on research they had conducted to determine the potential of keyword searching as a reasonable alternative to a built-in reference structure.[53] All name and subject access points were taken from a sample of records and were searched in *Library of Congress Name Authorities* and *Library of Congress Subject Headings*. Records for headings not found were eliminated. The "see" references suggested by both authorities were taken to be alternate forms to be searched. The researchers then checked all alternate forms against the bibliographic record from which the heading had been taken to determine whether the keywords in the alternate forms could be found anywhere in the record. A "success" required that every keyword of an alternate form heading be found somewhere in the record. Forty-six percent of the alternate form "author" headings (i.e., not counting names as subjects) were found represented in the bibliographic records (i.e., 46 percent of the references would be "unnecessary" in a system with keyword searching of *entire records*, but the remaining 54 percent would still be necessary). This cannot be compared with Thomas' findings, because the latter study included right-hand truncation possibilities and did not include searching of the entire record, but only of the authorized heading. The authors concluded that keyword searching, while being a powerful retrieval technique, cannot compensate for a lack of authority reference structure. (The subject findings of this study are discussed below.)

In 1987 Watson and Taylor reported findings from a study to determine which parts of the reference structure in LC authority records would be necessary to maintain in an online environment with automatic right-hand truncation and keyword searching.[54] A sample of personal names and a sample of corporate names were drawn from the LC online authority file. The researchers found that 68.3 percent of the personal name records and 25.5 percent of the corporate name records contained no references. (Statistics collected by James from LC's authority file in June 1985 showed that 63.7 percent of personal name records and 27.5 percent of corporate name records contained no references.)[55]

Watson and Taylor then categorized the references present to determine whether any would be "unnecessary" for searching purposes in an online environment as described above. They found that 41.5 percent of the personal name references and 21.9 percent of the corporate name references would be "unnecessary." The two figures cannot be combined, because the personal and corporate name samples were drawn separately so that each would contain 400 items. Thus, they represent different proportions of the universe. The 46 percent references found "unnecessary" by Jamieson, Dolan, and Declerck included both personal and corporate names without distinction and thus cannot be compared. By using known proportions of personal and corporate names in the LC authority file, Watson and Taylor concluded that about 65 percent of the name authority file would not be necessary for searching purposes in an online, keyword-searchable, right-hand truncation environment.

Watson and Taylor observed that use of name authority records by catalogers for authority control purposes had not been researched. In an effort to respond to this need, Dickson and Zadner conducted such a study. They found that for resolution of conflicts, the bibliographic file was much more useful than the authority file. Their work is reported elsewhere in this issue. It should be pointed out here that determining that many name authority records are not needed for searching purposes does not preclude the need for them in the process of automatic validation of names on bibliographic records and for other authority control functions, as will be discussed later in this review.

AUTHORITY CONTROL FOR WORKS

Most of the research and other work on authority control has discussed names. There has also been a smattering of work concerning subject authority control (see discussion below). An area that has only begun to be explored is authority control of works. Traditionally, works have been brought together in catalogs through choice of the same main entry and, if title is not main entry, the same title. When titles of different versions of the same work differ, an authority record may be created for the work, and one title may be chosen as the access point to be used on the bibliographic records involved, with a reference from alternate titles. The system breaks down when cataloging rules change between publication of versions of works (e.g., main entry under editor for the original version of the work, but under title for the reprint). Authority records are not made in such situations. It is assumed that the user will find the two records together, because an added entry has been made for what was previously the main entry. However, there is no explicit authority control in such situations as there is for names, subjects, and series.

The system also breaks down for some kinds of relationships between and among works. For example, translations are given authority control, but editions are only identified with previous ones on bibliographic records. Serials represent another case where authority control theory is not at work. Serials have fields in bibliographic records that are used to show relationships between them, while series have authority records to show these relationships. In most systems bibliographic files and authority files must be searched in different ways, and users are expected somehow to know the difference between serials and series.

Relationships between and among works are just beginning to be given attention in research. McNellis in 1985 attempted to learn what proportion of a research library's collection existed in multiple physical manifestations in the bibliographic universe.[56] She had difficulty determining what should be considered a "manifestation" due to lack of previously established definitions and theory in the area. She settled upon a fairly restrictive definition that included reprints, photocopies, publications at a later date that included only exactly the same information (e.g., no changes in introduction), etc. She found that about 26 percent of her sample existed in multiple manifestations. Although it is known that title changes exist in such situations, none were found in McNellis's sample.

Tillett's dissertation in 1987 defined seven categories of bibliographic relationships.[57] She gave attention to careful definition of these relationships and included lengthy lists of the types of items that fall into each category. For the most part, the category that Tillett called "equivalence relationships" matched the definition used by McNellis. Tillett looked for the presence of these categories in the MARC database of the Library of Congress. The relationships were identified both through MARC tags or identified text strings and through a sampling of "500" general notes. Because any one bibliographic record can exhibit more than one relationship, and because the counting was done for each kind of relationship separately, it was not possible to determine what proportion of all bibliographic records exhibit one or more relationships of some kind. However, there was an estimated total of 2,143,256 relationships identified in a database of 2,854,252 records. Thus, it can be seen that bibliographic relationships exist in large enough numbers to warrant attention to authority control for works.

Smith wrote in 1986 about series authority control in an online system.[58] While the article largely was concerned with implementation of series authority control in a particular system, Smith brought out some salient points for this area. She pointed out that author/title series forms may not be able to be handled in the same way as title series forms if the system expects names to be separate from titles. She also discussed what she called the "series/serial conundrum" – the fact that in most libraries serials are treated differently from series. Volume holdings may be displayed with the catalog record for a serial, but for monographic series may be available only in the records for the individual monographs. She pointed out that users approach the catalog with citations that often do not aid them in distinguishing between series and serials.

Smiraglia has completed research in the area of uniform titles. He found that title variations do appear for musical works in significant proportions. His work is reported elsewhere in this issue.

AUTHORITY CONTROL FOR SUBJECTS

Much of the theoretical literature on subject headings deals with the adequacy of currently used subject heading systems, discussing the adequacy/inadequacy of the terminology, the numbers of headings provided, and the adequacy/inadequacy of related, broader, and narrower term references. There is much less about authority control of subject headings on bibliographic records.

Tillett reported in her review a study conducted by students at the University of California, Berkeley, in 1972 on the subject headings in the Berkeley catalogs as compared to *Library of Congress Subject Headings* (LCSH).[59] They found that the Berkley subject headings were 1 percent out-of-date, 5 percent were unauthorized, and 40 percent were exact matches.

In 1980 O'Neill and Aluri examined subject heading fields of a sample of OCLC records and identified four major categories of errors.[60] O'Neill and Vizine-Goetz extended the O'Neill/Aluri study in 1982.[61] They reported that maintenance of a subject authority file for individual subfields, rather than for complete subject headings, would greatly reduce the size and complexity of the file. They estimated that there were nearly a half million different complete headings, but less than one hundred thousand unique subfields. Both studies found that the majority of errors fell into the following categories, listed from most common to least common:

1. Inconsistencies in spacing, punctuation, and capitalization;
2. Typographical and minor spelling errors;
3. Invalid form for heading;
4. Incorrect MARC tag or subfield code.[62]

O'Neill and Vizine-Goetz finally described an algorithm to be used for correcting errors in the first two categories and for flagging possible errors of the last two types for review.

Miller in 1984 discussed the need for authority control in the retrospective conversion process.[63] While much of the article explained the process used by Blackwell North America, and while Miller also discussed name authority control, there were some useful points made concerning subject authority control. Miller stated that the editorial staff had found that the category consisting of typographical and minor spelling errors "constitutes the largest portion of exceptions or nonmatches through the system."[64] No empirical data are given, but this is consistent with the O'Neill studies, because the editorial staff likely would not see O'Neill's most common category, as such errors would be corrected automatically by the system. Miller also observed that even when a heading matches a "see" reference, the change may not be automatic, because some unused terms refer to more than one authorized heading, and editors have to handle these.

In 1985 Ludy reported on use of an LC Subject Authority File (SAF) tape in MARC format to validate subjects in the catalog at Ohio State University.[65] The LC tape was for the year 1981, and the application was made in 1984; thus, there were a few problems with headings in the catalog representing newer versions of forms in the LC SAF. When the matching program was complete, 10 percent of the catalog headings had matched exactly with a heading/subdivision string in the SAF. Ludy reported that prior to the match, 21 percent of the catalog headings had been flagged as "verified." It is not clear whether these were included in the matching program. In any case, one of the reasons for so few matches is that the SAF does not contain every possible authorized heading/subdivision combination. Ludy commented:

. . . there are more than 500 authorized free-floating subdivisions, each of which can be combined with many established headings. In addition, geographic names may be used as subdivisions with 70 percent of headings, making the number of unique headings highly expandable.[66]

Assumption cannot be made that a subdivision used under one heading is authorized under all others, because there are restrictions in LCSH on use of many "free-floating" subdivisions. It might, however, be possible to program a validation process to check for the code that allows geographic subdivision and then validate such headings against verified geographic name subdivisions.

Frost and Dede reported in 1987 on a study to determine the degree to which topical and geographic subject heading strings from the University of Michigan Library's card catalog matched such strings as constructed in the 10th edition of LCSH (LCSH 10).[67] They also attempted to determine whether conflicting headings can be converted through automated authority control or whether they require human judgment. The researchers found that 44 percent of the subject headings strings, including subdivisions, matched exactly. Of the headings without subdivisions, 88.4 percent matched LCSH 10 exactly, but only 23 percent of the headings with subdivisions matched exactly. Three percent of main headings matched "see" references in LCSH 10 (although some of these had subdivisions). Six and a half percent of the main headings could not be found in LCSH 8, 9, or 10.

The reason for the great difference between the matching found by Frost/Dede and that found by Ludy is unclear. Ludy did not say whether headings from the two files were "normalized." It is possible that MARC tags, subfield codes, and spacing did not match in the Ohio State project. Such considerations would not have affected matches in the Frost/Dede study. It is also possible that there had been differences in the amount of manual authority control applied to subjects in the two libraries through the years.

Some work has also been done on the reference structure of subject authority control. Miller commented briefly upon the Blackwell North America system's ability to generate an authority file by copying all authority records matched during the authority control editing process.[68] In addition, the system "deblinds" all "see also from" references. Ludy reported that for the 410,000 unique subject headings in the OSU file, 70,576 "see-also" links were established, and 48,737 "see from" references were added and linked.[69] She commented that this restored a service that had been present in the card catalog before they went online. Jamieson, Dolan, and Declerck, in the study summarized above under "Reference Structure and Users' Needs," looked at whether keyword searching of bibliographic records would be as effective as maintaining a reference structure.[70] For subject headings they found that 73.5 percent of the alternate forms for name subject headings and 69.6 percent of the alternate forms for topical subject headings could *not* be found as keywords in the bibliographic records.

Palmer reported in 1986 a study in which he investigated subject authority control practices in nine libraries of varying types and sizes.[71] He also looked at chosen LC subject headings in each library to determine the effect of authority control practices. The three largest libraries were generally successful in updating changed headings and in providing "see" references, but they did not provide "see also" references. The six smaller libraries had few "see" references, and no "see also" references. In general in these smaller libraries, older materials were found under old headings, and new materials were placed under new headings with no references. Palmer called for research to determine whether patrons suffer from lack of subject authority control.

NEED FOR AUTHORITY FILES

There has been some discussion as to the need for authority files and at what level they are needed. Tillett mentioned two studies that had looked at authority files in libraries.[72] They showed that some libraries provided rigorous control while other libraries had no authority files. Young, whose study was conducted in 1974, suggested that the larger a library was, the more an authority file was needed.[73] Mosey's study, completed in 1980, showed a variety of practices in OCLC libraries with variations analyzed by type and size of library.[74] Both studies are now overshadowed by the fact that many libraries found it necessary to begin authority files in order to implement AACR 2 in 1981. Size of library is apparently still a factor, however, at least for subject authority files. In Palmer's study mentioned earlier, the six smaller libraries had no authority files.[75]

Ludy and Rogers[76] prepared in 1984 a counterargument to a statement made in 1983 by Stevenson[77] that the local authority file was becoming obsolete. They observed that as long as libraries have local catalogs, there must be local authority control. They discussed the shifting of some authority work to a higher hierarchical level (i.e., use of LC authority records through a network), but pointed out that only 20 percent of the headings in their nearly 100-year-old catalog had matched names on LC's tapes. They also pointed out that authority work necessary for original cataloging now requires integration with the union catalog of one's network, as well as with the local catalog. Finally, they suggested that while the *passive* local authority file has perhaps become obsolete, the interactive one has not.

Tillett reported in 1985 her preliminary analysis of an opinion poll on authority control that was circulated to the Library and Information Technology Association (LITA) membership in 1984.[78] Among the questions was one about using online resource authority files (i.e., available through networks for searching only). Even though there were many individual specific complaints, "the overwhelming response on the LITA poll was elation at having such a resource and praise for a tool that was found to be extremely valuable and useful."[79] Tillett also commented, "It was clear from the Dallas ALA Conference that there is a resurgent interest in authority control as more libraries actually begin their own online catalogs . . ."[80]

TECHNOLOGICAL CONSIDERATIONS

In 1985 Taylor, Maxwell, and Frost described and analyzed the various methods of automated authority control that were then available.[81] The categories identified were authority file processing, authority files online but unlinked to bibliographic files, and authority systems integrated with a system's bibliographic database.

Within these categories a number of variant approaches were analyzed.

McDonald in 1985 compared authority control to corporate world database administration and the use of the "data dictionary" in the data-processing industry.[82] Data dictionaries are used to control the representation of data and to help provide integrity and consistency. McDonald asserted that the function is the same as that called authority control in libraries. He then outlined the advantages of online linkage of "an authority control system with an online catalog":[83] (1) heading validation; (2) heading error flagging; (3) search term switching; (4) display of related terms; (5) reduction in data storage requirements; and (6) global change abilities. Advantage number 5 is based on the assumption that headings in authority records are used on more than one bibliographic record and that a number links the two so that the heading is not repeated on bibliographic records. It is true for subjects that a main heading is almost always used more than once (although there are no data about whether most main heading/subdivision combinations are used more than once); but since research has shown that two-thirds of personal names appear in a catalog only once and that two-thirds of non-subject access points are for personal names, there is a need to be cautious about accepting the validity of the assertion of reduced data storage requirements. (See also the reference to file size in the discussion of Epstein's article below.)

A problem with this article is that McDonald misconstrued the work of other writers. For example, he quoted Malinconico as saying, "the integrity of the elements of a cataloging record is an anachronistic concern of the precomputer age."[84] McDonald then proceeded to argue with this "view." Anyone who has read Malinconico knows that he is one of the strongest advocates of quality automated authority control. The entire sentence from which the quote was taken reads, "A simplistic notion that seems to be gaining popular acceptance suggests that the integrity of the access elements of a cataloging record is an anachronistic concern of the precomputer age."[85] Malinconico then explains why this "notion" is misleading.

While McDonald was describing the virtues of an ideal automated authority control system, Epstein was wondering if it was a "hidden time bomb."[86] Her article (in two parts) discussed problems that have been encountered in automated authority control enterprises. Subject headings have not always been carefully coded to indicate the source, resulting in headings being validated against the wrong authority file (e.g., validation using LCSH, when MeSH headings from the National Library of Medicine should have been used). Retrospective conversion projects have introduced outdated headings into a system as "new" ones. Most automated authority control systems at the time she wrote were based on use of headings derived from bibliographic records rather than from authority records. In Part II Epstein discussed automated authority control beyond the level of validating headings from new records against headings already in the bibliographic system. She pointed out that use of authority files has implications for disk storage space:

> With up to three authority records for every four title records, and authority records 75 percent as long as title records, it is apparent that a library can increase the disk storage space needed for a local integrated system by close to 50 percent of that needed for the storage of title records alone.[87]

Epstein also discussed the problems of updating the authority file, and of processing LC's file if one subscribes to it on one's own. For some public libraries, she noted, there may be a problem of "losing" books that have been shelved alphabetically by author's last name if automated authority control "flips" the name.

On the assumption that the technological problems would be worked out, Franklin conducted a study in 1987 to determine what proportion of name headings would be validated if automated authority control were put into effect.[88] Two separate concerns addressed were the proportions of names that would be validated for ongoing current cataloging, and the proportions of names that would be validated in applying automated authority control to retrospective records. In the first instance she found that 92.6 percent of name headings from current cataloging matched an AACR 2 heading or a reference to such a heading. About 1.1 percent matched pre-AACR 2 headings or had typographical errors, and the remaining 6.2 percent were not in the LC authority file. In the retrospective matching sample, about 65 percent of the headings matched an AACR 2 heading or a reference to such a heading, while 6.3 percent matched pre-AACR 2 headings or contained errors, and 28.7 percent were not in the authority file. Franklin observed that the difference between her 65 percent match and the 20 percent match reported by Ludy and Rogers (discussed above under "Need for Authority Files") might be explained partially by the much smaller collection used in the Franklin study. A more positive reason suggested was that two years had passed and many more headings had been added to the authority file.

CONCLUSION

Clearly, much progress has been made in the seven years since Svenonius challenged us to research authority control questions.[89] Studies on the need for tying together variant forms of names and terms, as well as articles on how to cope with the lack of such linkages, indicate that authority control is certainly needed. The questions Svenonius asked about how linkage information is to be accessed, whether all linkage information should be contained in an authority file, and the means for interfacing authority and bibliographic files have been examined to some extent, although the answers are not yet clear. Some advocate full MARC authority records for every heading, while others question the cost-effectiveness and efficiency of this approach. Perhaps these questions remain unanswered because Svenonius's remaining question, that of efficient file design, has yet to be examined; and the answers to the preceding questions quite possibly hinge on this one. Could it be that it is time to consider the file design envisioned by Gorman in the late 1970s?[90] He saw a design in which physical items would be represented in unique records, unencumbered by access points, but linked to each record that represents one of the persons, corporate bodies, works, and subjects that are associated with that physical item. In addition, records representing persons, bodies, works, and subjects would be linked to each other as needed. In such a world the conflicts we now have of some linkage information being held in the authority file and the remainder being held in the bibliographic file would be resolved, for the two files would be one.

REFERENCES

1. Larry Auld, "Authority Control: An Eighty-Year Review," *Library Resources & Technical Services* 26 (October/December 1982): 319-330.
2. Barbara B. Tillett, "Automated Authority Files and Authority Control: A Survey of the Literature," seminar paper, Graduate School of Library and Information Science, University of California, Los Angeles, June 1982; with corrections and additions, October 1982.
3. Auld, "Authority Control," pp. 325-326.
4. Helen F. Schmierer, "The Relationship of Authority Control to the Library Catalog," *Illinois Libraries* 62 (September 1980): 599-603.
5. Martin Runkle, "Authority in On-Line Catalogs," *Illinois Libraries* 62 (September 1980): 603-606.
6. S. Michael Malinconico, "Bibliographic Data Base Organization and Authority File Control," *Wilson Library Bulletin* 54 (September 1979): 36-45. (Also published in *Authority Control: The Key to Tomorrow's Catalog:* proceedings of the 1979 Library and Information Technology Association Institutes, edited by Mary W. Ghikas, Phoenix, Ariz.: Oryx Press, 1982, pp. 1-8.)
7. S. Michael Malinconico, "Mass Storage Technology and File Organization," *Journal of Library Automation* 13 (June 1980): 77-87.
8. Kathryn Luther Henderson, "Great Expectations: the Authority Control Connection," *Illinois Libraries* 65 (May 1983): 334-336.
9. Henriette D. Avram, "Authority Control and Its Place," *Journal of Academic Librarianship* 9 (January 1984): 331-335.
10. Doris Hargrett Clack, "Authority Control: Issues and Answers," *Technical Services Quarterly* 3 (Fall 1985/Winter 1985-86): 127-140.
11. Doris Hargrett Clack, "On Becoming an Authority on Authorities: A Working Bibliography," *Florida Libraries* 33 (January/February 1983): 13-18.
12. Martin Runkle, "Authority Control: A Library Director's View," *Journal of Academic Librarianship* 12 (July 1986): 145-146.
13. Ibid., p. 145.
14. Ibid., p. 146.
15. Pat Oddy, "Name Authority Files," *Catalogue & Index*, no. 82 (Autumn 1986): 1, 3-4.
16. Ibid., p. 3.
17. Ibid., p. 4.
18. Tillett, "Automated Authority Files," pp. 53-54.
19. Phyllis A. Richmond, "Research Possibilities in the Machine Readable Catalog: Use of the Catalog to Study Itself," *Journal of Academic Librarianship* 2 (November 1976): 224-229 (as cited in Tillett, "Automated Authority Files," p. 53).
20. Brett Butler, "Closing Remarks" (in *Authority Control: The Key to Tomorrow's Catalog*, p. 181-185; as cited in Tillett, "Automated Authority Files," p. 53).
21. R. Bruce Miller, "Authority Control in the Network Environment" (in

Authority Control: The Key to Tomorrow's Catalog, p. 36-52; as cited in Tillett, "Automated Authority Files," pp. 52-53).

22. Ake I. Koel, "Bibliographic Control at the Crossroads: Do We Get Our Money's Worth?" *Journal of Academic Librarianship* 7 (September 1981): 220-222 (as cited in Tillett, "Automated Authority Files," p. 52).

23. Jeanette Gail Mosey, "Name Authority Work in OCLC Libraries: A Survey of Practices and Expectations," Ph.D. diss., University of Southern California, 1980 (as cited in Tillett, "Automated Authority Files," p. 54).

24. Elaine Svenonius, "Directions for Research in Indexing, Classification, and Cataloging," *Library Resources & Technical Services* 25 (January/March 1981): 101.

25. Seymour Lubetzky and R. M. Hayes, "Bibliographic Dimensions in Information Cont[r]ol," *American Documentation* 20 (July 1969): 247-252.

26. Beecher Wiggins, "Cataloging: How Important Are Unique Access Points?" *RTSD Newsletter* 9 (no. 7, 1984): 88-89.

27. Ibid., p. 88.

28. Malinconico, "Mass Storage Technology" (as cited in Wiggins, "Cataloging," p. 89).

29. Nancy J. Williamson, "Is There a Catalog in Your Future? Access to Information in the Year 2006," *Library Resources & Technical Services* 26 (April 1982): 122-135 (as cited in Wiggins, "Cataloging," p. 89).

30. Auld, "Authority Control," p. 326. (This quotation is summarizing a concept expressed by Michael Gorman in "Authority Control in the Prospective Catalog," in *Authority Control: The Key to Tomorrow's Catalog*, pp. 166-180).

31. Tillett, "Automated Authority Files," p. 42. (The reference is to Seymour Lubetzky, *Principles of Cataloging*, Los Angeles, Calif.: Institute of Library Research, University of California, 1969.)

32. Tillett, "Automated Authority Files," pp. 42-43. (The references are to IFLA, International Office for UBC, *The International MARC Network: Bibliographic Study*, London, 1977, 28 p.; J. Poncet, "Authority Files in Machine Systems," in *The Interchange of Bibliographic Information in Machine Readable Form*, R. E. Coward and M. Yelland, eds., London: Library Association, 1975, pp. 96-98; S. Michael Malinconico, "The Library Catalog in a Computerized Environment," *The Nature and Future of the Catalog*, edited by Maurice J. Freedman and S. Michael Malinconico, Phoenix, Ariz.: Oryx Press, 1979, pp. 46-68.)

33. Robert H. Burger, "Artificial Intelligence and Authority Control," *Library Resources & Technical Services* 28 (October/December 1984): 337-345.

34. Charles R. Hildreth, *Online Public Access Catalogs: The User Interface*. Dublin, Ohio: OCLC, 1982, pp. 120-121.

35. Melinda L. Shore, "Variation Between Personal Name Headings and Title Page Usage," *Cataloging & Classification Quarterly* 4 (Summer 1984): 1-11.

36. Elizabeth E. Fuller, "Variation in Personal Names in the Catalog," master's paper, Graduate Library School, University of Chicago, 1986.

37. Cathy Ann Elias and C. James Fair, "Name Authority Control in a Communication System," *Special Libraries* 74 (July 1983): 289-296.

38. Cathy Ann Elias, "Authority Control in a Communication System at Standard Oil (Indiana)," master's paper, Graduate Library School, University of Chicago, 1982.

39. Catherine E. Pasterczyk, "Russian Transliteration Variations for Searchers," *DATABASE* 8 (February 1985): 68-75.

40. Anne B. Piternick, "What's in a Name? Use of Names and Titles in Subject Searching," *DATABASE* 8 (December 1985): 22-28.

41. David M. Pilachowski and David Everett, "What's in a Name? Looking for People Online—Social Sciences," *DATABASE* 8 (August 1985): 47-65.

42. David M. Pilachowski and David Everett, "What's in a Name? Looking for People Online—Current Events," *DATABASE* 9 (April 1986): 43-50.

43. David Everett and David M. Pilachowski, "What's in a Name? Looking for People Online—Humanities," *DATABASE* 9 (October 1986): 26-34.

44. Bonnie Snow, "Caduceus: People in Medicine: Searching Names Online," *ONLINE* 10 (September 1986): 122-127.

45. Pasterczyk, "Russian Transliteration," p. 75.

46. Max J. Evans, "Authority Control: An Alternative to the Record Group Concept," *American Archivist* 49 (Summer 1986): 249-261.

47. Ibid., p. 255.

48. Ibid.

49. Arlene G. Taylor, "Authority Files in Online Catalogs: an Investigation of Their Value," *Cataloging & Classification Quarterly* 4 (Spring 1984): 1-17.

50. Ibid., pp. 9-10.

51. Karen G. Roughton and David A. Tyckoson, "Browsing with Sound: Sound-Based Codes and Automated Authority Control," *Information Technology and Libraries* 4 (June 1985): 130-136.

52. Catherine M. Thomas, "Authority Control in Manual Versus Online Catalogs: an Examination of "See" References," *Information Technology and Libraries* 3 (December 1985): 393-398.

53. Alexis J. Jamieson, Elizabeth Dolan, and Luc Declerck, "Keyword Searching vs. Authority Control in an Online Catalog," *Journal of Academic Librarianship* 12 (November 1986): 277-283.

54. Mark R. Watson and Arlene G. Taylor, "Implications of Current Reference Structures for Authority Work in Online Environments," *Information Technology and Libraries* 6 (March 1987): 10-19.

55. John R. James, [senior automation planning specialist at the Library of Congress], personal communication, November 1985.

56. Claudia Houk McNellis, "Describing Reproductions: Multiple Physical Manifestations in the Bibliographical Universe," *Cataloging & Classification Quarterly* 5 (Spring 1985): 35-48.

57. Barbara Ann Barnett Tillett, "Bibliographic Relationships: Toward a Conceptual Structure of Bibliographic Information Used in Cataloging," Ph.D.

diss., Graduate School of Library and Information Science, University of California, Los Angeles, 1987.

58. Barbara G. Smith, "Online Series Authority Control in the Integrated Library System," *Technicalities* 6 (July 1986): 3-5.

59. Tillett, "Automated Authority Files," p. 20 (reference is to Judy Todd, "Summary Report of Student Studies of the Subject Headings Used in the University of California, Berkeley, Subject Catalog: Final Report," Institute of Library Research, University of California, Berkeley, July 1973, 10 p.).

60. Edward T. O'Neill and Rao Aluri, *A Method for Correcting Typographical Errors in Subject Headings in OCLC Records*, Report no. OCLC/OPR/RR-80/3, Columbus, Ohio: OCLC, 1980.

61. Edward T. O'Neill and Diane Vizine-Goetz, "Computer Generation of a Subject Authority File," *Proceedings of the ASIS Annual Meeting* 19 (1982): 220-223.

62. Ibid., p. 220.

63. Dan Miller, "Authority Control in the Retrospective Conversion Process," *Information Technology and Libraries* 3 (September 1984): 286-292.

64. Ibid., p. 288.

65. Lorene E. Ludy, "OSU Libraries' Use of Library of Congress Subject Authorities File," *Information Technology and Libraries* 4 (June 1985): 155-160.

66. Ibid., p. 159.

67. Carolyn O. Frost and Bonnie A. Dede, "Subject Heading Compatibility Between LCSH and Catalog Files of a Large Research Library: a Suggested Model for Analysis," report to the Council on Library Resources, October 1987.

68. Miller, "Authority Control in the Retrospective Conversion Process," p. 291.

69. Ludy, "OSU Libraries' Use," pp. 157-158.

70. Jamieson, Dolan, and Declerck, "Keyword Searching," p. 279.

71. Joseph W. Palmer, "Subject Authority Control and Syndetic Structure — Myth and Realities: an Inquiry into Certain Subject Heading Practices and Some Questions About Their Implications," *Cataloging & Classification Quarterly* 7 (Winter 1986): 71-95.

72. Tillett, "Automated Authority Files," p. 24.

73. Young, Juanita Minter, "Name Authority Files: an Exploratory Study," master's paper, Graduate School of Library and Information Science, University of California, Los Angeles, 1974 (as cited in Tillett, "Automated Authority Files," p. 24).

74. Mosey, "Name Authority Work" (as cited in Tillett, "Automated Authority Files," p. 24).

75. Palmer, "Subject Authority Control," p. 88.

76. Lorene E. Ludy and Sally A. Rogers, "Authority Control in the Online Environment," *Information Technology and Libraries* 3 (September 1984): 262-266.

77. Gordon Stevenson, "Descriptive Cataloging in 1982," *Library Resources & Technical Services* 27 (July/September 1983): 262.

78. Barbara B. Tillett, "1984 Automated Authority Control Opinion Poll: A Preliminary Analysis," *Information Technology and Libraries* 4 (June 1985): 171-178.

79. Tillett, "1984 Automated Authority Control Opinion Poll," p. 174.

80. Ibid., p. 178.

81. Arlene G. Taylor, Margaret F. Maxwell, and Carolyn O. Frost, "Network and Vendor Authority Systems," *Library Resources & Technical Services* 29 (April/June 1985): 195-205.

82. David R. McDonald, "Data Dictionaries, Authority Control, and Online Catalogs: A New Perspective," *Journal of Academic Librarianship* 11 (September 1985): 219-222.

83. Ibid., p. 221.

84. Ibid., p. 220.

85. Malinconico, "Bibliographic Data Base Organization," p. 3.

86. Susan Baerg Epstein, "Automated Authority Control: A Hidden Time-bomb? Part I," *Library Journal* 110 (November 1, 1985): 36-37; "Part II," *Library Journal* 111 (January 1986): 55-56.

87. Epstein, p. 55.

88. Laurel F. Franklin, "Preparing for Automated Authority Control: a Projection of Name Headings Verified," *Journal of Academic Librarianship* 13 (September 1987): 205-208.

89. Svenonius, "Directions for Research," p. 101.

90. Gorman, "Authority Control in the Prospective Catalog," pp. 167-168, 172-174.

Authority Control and the Authority File: A Functional Evaluation of LCNAF on RLIN

Jean Dickson
Patricia Zadner

SUMMARY. The costs of authority control are high and the information provided in authority files is often duplicated in separate bibliographic files. Librarians need to examine the compatibility of traditional methods of authority control with the advanced capabilities of current computer systems. This study investigates the actual use of the Library of Congress Name Authority File (LCNAF) by catalogers in an RLIN member library. Results show that some aspects of authority control could be expedited by changes in cataloging practice and search software.

INTRODUCTION AND LITERATURE SURVEY

In several recent articles, librarians have challenged the traditional assumptions about authority work in light of current and predicted capabilities of online public access catalogs and their associated authority files. Authority work entails several purposes:

1. creation of uniform headings (access points) to ensure collocation of all closely related works under uniform headings;
2. creation of links (usually in the form of cross-references) to

Jean Dickson is Senior Assistant, Monograph Cataloger at the State University of New York at Buffalo. Patricia Zadner is Associate Librarian, Serials Cataloger at the State University of New York at Buffalo.

The research for this study was conducted by Dickson and Zadner; the article was written by Dickson.

57

lead the searcher from variant forms of the heading to the established form;
3. provision of adequate information to distinguish one established heading from another similar heading.

Today there appear to be few adherents of the view that online catalogs need no authority control because truncation, keyword, and Boolean searching will bring together all variations of any name. However, there is some concern about the large amount of time and resources being consumed by authority work, at a time when many research libraries continue to backlog books. In 1986, Nadine Baer and Karl Johnson surveyed American college and university libraries as to their need for and use of authority control. While most of the 171 libraries responding either did not answer the questions pertaining to staff hours spent maintaining authority control or responded that they did not keep track of them, the data from those who did respond shows an interesting pattern. The libraries with online authority files spent at least twice as many professional hours per week as those with manual files, and the online "linked" authority files seemed to require more maintenance time than either manual or online unlinked files, when professional, paraprofessional and clerical hours are added together.[1] There are a number of possible explanations of this phenomenon. Perhaps the librarians provide more extensive and effective control in the online files; perhaps online index displays in their local bibliographic files have revealed inconsistencies which demand increased authority work; perhaps the requirement for MARC tagging, subfield indicators, etc., slows down work; or perhaps participation in NACO or other shared authority files has motivated librarians to conduct more exhaustive research and closer review of authority records.

The Library of Congress also conducted a survey in 1986, to research the costs of NACO membership to the member libraries. The cost per record created ranged from $3.15 to almost $63, while the average (mean) cost was $14.67. Eighty percent of the libraries responding had a cost of $20.00 or less.[2] On the other hand, a few of the libraries also cited the costs of creating non-NACO authority records: on average, $7.30 per record, or about half the cost of the average NACO record. These costs reflect overhead and communications as well as staff time. Many of the libraries responding to the NACO questionnaire cited "additional review" and "extra searching" as factors accounting for the extra time spent on NACO records.[3]

Arlene Taylor, Catherine Thomas, Mark Watson, and others have conducted research to test whether current authority files accomplish the purposes listed above, whether they have weathered the transition from a card format to a computer-held database. A logical conclusion that can be drawn from these studies is that much of the work which has gone into the Library of Congress authority file has been unnecessary or redundant for certain online environments.

In particular, Taylor's article showed that the erroneous searches entered by patrons in Northwestern University's LUIS system matched Library of Congress Name Authorities File cross-references only 6.4% of the time.[4] She suggested that library users would have found what they wanted more often if the library focused on software enhancements, such as spelling checkers, which would correct a much larger percentage of the failed search arguments (40.1%). Furthermore, she found that 57.5% of the subset of personal names which were represented by LC authority records were in records that contained no cross-references.[5]

Catherine Thomas' study looked at a sample of 426 manual cross-references at the University of California at San Diego to see whether they would be necessary in the online system, MELVYL, where automatic right truncation and keyword searching were available to patrons and staff. She concluded that 47% of the references were superfluous for the MELVYL environment: they only inverted multiple surnames or corporate-name word order, or involved only differences in forename fullness.[6]

In a follow-up of these studies, Mark Watson and Arlene Taylor examined a random sample of corporate and personal name authority records from the Library of Congress Name Authority File (hereafter, LCNAF). They found that 68% of the personal name authority records (PNARs) and 25.5% of the corporate name authority records (CNARs) contained *no* references.[7] Among the remaining authority records, another 14.5% of total PNARs and 11.4% of CNARs contained only unnecessary references. Further,

16% of the cross-references in necessary PNARs, and 15.3% in necessary CNARs were considered unnecessary.[8] The authors concluded that the LCNAF could be reduced to less than 35% of its current size with no loss of information, assuming the availability of keyword searching and automatic right truncation.[9]

A study conducted by three researchers at the University of Western Ontario asked whether keyword and Boolean search capabilities could substitute for cross-reference links to authorized headings. As experimental search terms, they used the "nonpreferred terms" provided as see- and see-from references in the LCNAF and the Library of Congress Subject Headings list. They concluded that even an online catalog with Boolean, keyword, and truncation capabilities needs a cross-reference structure. There was no effort to discover how often users actually input the nonpreferred terms that were provided.[10]

Are we in fact making the best use of our human and computer resources? Are we missing the boat by trying to force the computer-held authority file to mimic the functioning of the card authority file? Watson and Taylor asked several questions about catalogers' use of the LC authority file. They pointed out, for example that the 670 fields (source notes) provide clues to catalogers who need to decide whether the name on the item being cataloged matches the heading on an authority record. The same information, though, is available in almost all cases in the bibliographic file already, and in more complete form. They theorized other notes, including historical information on corporate bodies (now no longer being added at the Library of Congress), or dates of birth and/or death, place of employment, degrees granted, etc., might be essential to catalogers. "How often does the worst-case scenario occur? In other words, how often will an examination of the headings in the authority file, along with the bibliographic records associated with those headings, lead to a complete dead end?"[11]

METHODOLOGY

We set out to investigate this and related questions about how we, as catalogers, actually use the LCNAF. We hoped to ascertain which facets of authority work (as it is currently done) are necessary and well served by the authority file, and which are not.

To this end, we kept records of all our searches for personal and corporate names (including authors and a few subjects) that we conducted on RLIN in April and May 1987, and continued through June for corporate names only. We recorded both the text of each search and a number of facts about it: the date of publication and language of the item in which the name was found, whether the name matched the heading (1XX field), the heading with qualifier, or a cross-reference (4XX or 5XX), whether the record included cross-references, whether the name was indistinct (either appearing in an indistinct authority record or seeming to match more than one record in the authority file), and then, if it was *not* found in the authority file, whether it was found in member or LC copy in the bibliographic, "books/serials" file of RLIN. At the end we had a list of 404 personal names and 179 corporate names. We did not record duplicates, geographic names, author-title, series, or uniform title searches.

At SUNY Buffalo, we do our cataloging on RLIN and produce cards for our local catalog; as yet we have an automated system only for circulation. Zadner collected most of the corporate names, and Dickson collected all of the personal names. Zadner's materials tend to be primarily recent and in English; Dickson's are predominantly foreign-language, almost never any non-Roman, and somewhat older (Table 1). Our initial breakdown (Table 2) used 1981 date of publication as a watershed, to approximate the date of cataloging corresponding to the Library of Congress' implementation of AACR2, but we later felt that a more important dividing line might be the advent of MARC (more on this later).

TABLE 1:   Languages of Sources of Names

	English	German	French	Other languages
Personal Names	35%	45%	12%	8%
Corporate Names	76%	8%	4%	12%

TABLE 2:   Dates of Publication of Sources of Names

	1981 and later	1980 and earlier
Personal Names	59.5%	40.5%
Corporate Names	80.5%	19.5%

RLIN Searching

Readers who are unfamiliar with RLIN's search capabilities need to know that one may use the "fin pe" command to search for the exact form of name, or "fin pn" to search a truncated form of the name, i.e., surname, first initial(s). The authority file index thus accessed includes all the 100, 400, and rarely 500 fields in the LC authority records. In searching for corporate names, one can use "fin cp" and truncate with the "#" symbol, when desired, or look for keywords by means of the "fin cw" command. These commands take one into the index that holds the 11X, 41X, and 51X fields of authority records.

HYPOTHESES

We hypothesized that we would make maximal use of the LCNAF. After all, unlike the patrons, we catalogers approach the terminal with the book or serial in hand which serves as the basis for establishing names, at least in theory. Moreover, our conceptual model of the file is probably very similar to that of its designers, who are also technical services librarians. We thought that by means of skilled use and educated guesses we would find virtually everything that was available.

In particular, we expected:

1. to have a much higher percentage of "hits" on the 4XX fields than the library users, 6.4% as found in Taylor's 1984 article. Our entries should more often match the 4XX fields, because

these variations in form usually are drawn from title-page manifestations.

2. Our sample should include a higher number of records with 4XX and 5XX fields (see-references and see-also-references) than the random samples because famous and/or prolific authors would be more heavily represented. Works by the more famous authors would be more translated and reissued, and thus show a number of variations in form of name.

3. Older materials would present a larger number of names which were either not online or had not yet been established in AACR2 form, and similarly, the pre-1968 English and pre-1970s foreign-language materials would present many names that would be absent or not established.

RESULTS

In general, we proved to be quite successful in retrieving headings. We found about two-thirds of the personal names and about three-quarters of the corporate names in the authority file (see Tables 3 and 4, and Pie Charts 1 and 2 in Appendix 1).

In harmony with Thomas' results: in 253 cases of 404 personal names (62.6%), right-end truncation of the form of name in the piece in hand would have insured a match with the 100 field (the established heading) in the authority record. In almost 15% of the names searched, the only differences were in subfields "d" or "c" or in middle initials/names. When we consider only the subset of successful searches (i.e., sections A and B of Pie Chart 1), the percentage is very high, 92.6%.

Truncation was, of course, significant in matching corporate name headings in all cases where qualifiers were involved. These accounted for 12.5% of the corporate names found in the LCNAF (see section B of Pie Chart 2). For example:

Form found in piece: Church Historical Society.
LCNAF 110 heading: Church Historical Society (U.S.)

In piece: Native American Center for the Living Arts
LCNAF 110: Native American Center for the Living Arts
(Niagara Falls, New York)

```
TABLE 3: Categories of Personal Names Searched

Found in the authority file:                    273    (67.5 %)
    Matches 100 field:       253   (62.6 %)
    Matches 400 field:        20   ( 4.9 %)
Found only in the bibliographic file:            76    (18.8 %)
    Matches LC heading:       32   ( 7.9 %)
    Matches RLIN member hdg.: 44   (10.8 %)
Not found in either file:                         55    (13.6 %)
    New to files              49   (12.1 %)
    Indistinct/unknown         6   ( 1.4 %)        _____

Total names searched:                           404    (100 %)
```

```
TABLE 4: Categories of Corporate Names Searched

Found in the authority file:                    142    (79 %)
    Matches 11X exactly         109      (61 %)
    Matches 11X plus qualifier   21      (12 %)
    Matches 41X                  12      ( 7 %)
Found only in bibliographic file:                 9    ( 5 %)
New to files:                                    28    (16 %)

Total names searched:                           179   (100 %)
```

In only one case was truncation of the name itself necessary to match a 41X field:

> In piece: Verband deutscher Bühnenschriftsteller
> LCNAF 110: Verband deutscher Bühnenschriftsteller und
> Komponisten.

(This may represent an earlier or later form of name.) More often, the longer form of name matches a 41X field, as in this example:

> In piece: Universidad Michoacana de San Nicolas de Hidalgo
> LCNAF 110: Universidad Michoacana.

The percentage of authority records found that had *no* cross-references (4XX or 5XX fields) was 45% of the personal names (122 out of a total of 273) and only 19% of the corporate names (27 out of 142 names found). Compare this to the 68.3% for personal names and 25.5% for corporate names reported in the Watson and

Taylor random sample study.[12] This confirmed our hypothesis about catalogers' use of the authority file.

Unlike Catherine Thomas, we did not look at the number and usefulness of cross-references; we just made a yes-or-no decision as to whether the records accessed contained cross-references. However, if we look at the data from a functional perspective, we see that we accessed the authority file through cross-references only 7.2% of the time, or 30 personal and corporate names out of 416 names found in the authority file. As a percentage of all the searches performed, access through the 4XXs or 5XXs becomes an even less important portion: 5.1% of all names. Surprisingly enough, this is not significantly better than the hypothetical success rate for library patrons reported in Taylor's 1984 article (6.4%).[13]

Within the category of personal names that matched the cross-references, 10 out of 20 (section B of Pie Chart 1) were variations to the right of the forename initial. For example:

Form found in piece: I. Aleksander
LCNAF 100 heading: Aleksander, Igor.

In piece: Ezekial Mphahlele
LCNAF 100: Mphahlele, Es'kia.

In piece: Dietrich von dem Werder
LCNAF 100: Werder, Diederich von dem, 1584-1657.

Seven of the names varied in forename fullness, two varied in forename spelling, and one (Bruder Grimm) was a collective name. Of the remaining ten names, four were compound surnames or appeared to be such, which Dickson entered under the wrong name element. For example, for S.A. Amu Djoleto, the established heading is "Djoleto, S. A. Amu (Solomon Alexander Amu), 1929-   " and not "Amu Djoleto, etc." as Dickson had guessed. Six of the names were different romanizations or different language forms of names. For example:

In piece: Mahmoud Bouayed
LCNAF 100: Bu Ayyad, Mahmud.

In piece: Friedrich der Grosse
LCNAF 100: Frederick II, King of Prussia, 1712-1786.

Similarly, only 3 corporate names matched inverted forms in 41X fields, as in:

> In piece: Colleges of Further and Higher Education Group of
>   the Library Association
> LCNAF 110: Library Association. Colleges of Further and
>   Higher Education Group.

> In piece: Annual Conference of the Canadian Council for
>   Southeast Asian Studies . . .
> LCNAF 111: Canadian Council for Southeast Asian Studies.
>   Conference . . .

In most cases we searched first under the larger body because we expected the new item to be established as a sub-body under AACR2.

Cross-references sometimes bring together variant spellings; we had only one example of access through such a reference:

> In piece: Koninklijke Vlaamsche Academie voor Wetens-
> chappen, Letteren en Schone Kunsten van Belgie
> LCNAF 110: Koninklijke Vlaamse Academie . . . (etc.)

We used the corporate name keyword search only rarely. In one case it saved Dickson a lot of searching for the "Nairobi World Conference on Women" (as it appeared as subject in a work). She found it by entering "fin cw nairobi world conference," which brought up the established heading: World Conference to Review and Appraise the Achievements of the United Nations Decade for Women (1985 : Nairobi, Kenya).

We expected to find strong correlations between the date of publication of the material being cataloged (as an approximation of the date of cataloging) and the percentage of names in their associated bibliographic records that were found in the LCNAF, and between the language of the publication and the percentage of names found in the LCNAF. The results of our investigation were ambiguous. Since the Library of Congress now bases authority decisions solely on evidence in MARC records, we decided that the most significant date would divide MARC from pre-MARC: 1968 for English-language materials, and 1972 for most other European languages. The results are tabulated in two four-square charts (Tables 5 and 6).

As for the notes and other information stored in the authority records to help catalogers distinguish similar names, we found very few cases in which the notes proved to be crucial. None of the

TABLE 5: Percentage of Personal Names Found in the LCNAF, by Category

English-language sources

78.9%	63.5%
(15 of 19)	(80 of 126)

"Old" ——————————————— "New"

66.7%	68.5%
(88 of 132)	(89 of 130)

Non-English-language sources

TABLE 6: Percentage of Corporate Names Found in the LCNAF, by Category

English-language sources

85.7%	85.0%
(6 of 7)	(113 of 133)

"Old" ——————————————— "New"

75.0%	65.5%
(6 of 8)	(19 of 29)

Non-English-language sources

(Horizontal axes represent date of publication of materials from which the names were drawn; vertical axes represent language of the materials.)

corporate names were distinguished in this way. Personal authors' dates of birth and death and the titles of publications seem to be the determining factors, along with the cataloger's general background knowledge.

Watson and Taylor mention that catalogers might use the bibliographic file itself for establishing a connection between the piece in hand and the other works of the author, as an alternative to the source notes and other information which is sometimes stored in authority records.[14] Intuitively we thought that our own use of the bibliographic file for authority work was quite heavy. We feel that if RLIN would provide author index screens, we would use the bibliographic file even more. Searching RLIN can be very time-consuming, particularly when the heading sought is not the main entry in the records displayed. In such cases, the cataloger often must examine each record in the RLIN cluster(s) by typing in a separate command. For the corporate names only 6 (i.e., category D on Pie Chart 2) out of the 36 not-found (i.e., category D plus E) were matched in the bibliographic file. With personal names we were more successful in the bibliographic file. Dickson found in the bibliographic file 76 out of 131 of the names not found in the LCNAF. Out of those 76 names, 44 were found only in member-contributed copy; the other 32 had been used in LC records but not established yet in AACR2 form. This result confirmed our expectation about our use of the books file.

We also used the bibliographic file to find some names for which we did not have a complete or official-looking form of the name in the piece in hand. For example, Zadner found a transliterated Japanese corporate name by truncating it to the first two words and browsing the bibliographic file until she found it, realizing then that the third word had been misspelled. In other cases, inverting word order or changing "of" to "on," or similar educated guesses resulted in hits.

Likewise, there were a few personal names which were found because of tangential search techniques, such as title-word searches. For example, the name "Mong Dsi" was on the title page of a German translation of a work by Mencius. Dickson was able to discover his true identity by means of a search for the editor's works, all of which concerned Mencius.

CONCLUSIONS

The information that catalogers use to perform authority control is diverse and diffuse. While our study shows that the authority file, in this case, the LCNAF, is the primary source of information, it is *not* the file of last resort. Conflicts are only rarely resolved by means of the authority file; it is the bibliographic file that unlocks the most complex searches. Network bibliographic files, such as RLIN and OCLC, and even paper bibliographic files (especially the National Union Catalog) include hundreds of thousands of records from many institutions and are often better able to resolve ambiguities and confusions because of their diversity and size.

Like library users, we have adapted to the tools provided. We "must separate the behavior that is an indication of underlying needs from the portion that is an adaptation to the systems we have constructed."[15] In our project, we succeeded in resolving two-thirds to three-quarters of the authority problems in the authority file, because that is where we looked first. In the overwhelming majority of those cases, we had the same form of name in the piece in hand as in LCNAF, or the form variation was in the right end of the name, e.g., dates, titles, or qualifiers, differences which were resolved by right-end truncation.

In almost all cases, the authority record holds the same information as the associated bibliographic record, but less of it. This implies that the RLIN bibliographic file could resolve almost all of the authority control problems if better access to bibliographic indexes were provided.

We do not suggest that authority work could be completely automated; human catalogers require a great deal of background and contextual information from both examination of the piece and memory to resolve problem cases. Nor would it be practical to eliminate all authority work, hoping that truncation, Boolean, and keyword searching capabilities would obviate the need for an established form of name. These more flexible search capabilities will not ensure collocation of all headings that serve as surrogates for same or related authors, subjects, etc.

Perhaps the creation and maintenance of a separate authority file is not the best alternative. A long-term solution may be the integration of bibliographic and authority files. In the short run, however, we have several suggestions for improved search capabilities on RLIN.

In the current RLIN software, access is (apparently) designed primarily for the purpose of interlibrary loan. The catalog screens display brief bibliographic descriptions and holdings of each particular edition of a work (see Appendix 2). A cataloger who wishes to research the headings and usage of names not assigned as the main entry in a work must access each record through a separate command, e.g., "dis 1 ful" and then, "dis 2 iaug ful" etc. Another problem in cataloging on RLIN is the separate access to the bibliographic and authority files. Ideally, one could flip back and forth between bibliographic and authority files with only one keystroke, and even save the authority record in a workspace and display it alongside the bibliographic record being revised or created.

If the index listing of records by a particular author were made visible to the searcher, one would need to access full records much less often, in fact, only when one wished to see the usage in particular records. If there were also the Boolean capability of limiting a search by "and-ing" a publication date or range of publication dates or a cataloging code (i.e., display only those records coded as AACR2 level), a great deal of time spent tediously paging through bibliographic records could be avoided.

Network databases have enabled librarians to make some important advances in authority work, both in understanding its importance in providing reliably inclusive collocation of headings and in application of higher standards of cataloging to facilitate sharing of bibliographic and authority records. Because each library can now count on Library of Congress and member copy, librarians can use their specializations more effectively; conversely, the demands on catalogers for more obscure subject and language expertise has grown.

While networks such as RLIN and OCLC may never approximate the user-friendly access of some local OPACs, because their databases are so huge and the uses to which they are put are so diverse, it is clear that their cataloging interface could be made much more effective for authority control.

BIBLIOGRAPHIC REFERENCES

1. Nadine L. Baer and Karl E. Johnson, "The State of Authority," *Information Technology and Libraries* 7, no. 2 (June 1988), pp. 139-153.

2. Randall K. Barry, *Report of the 1986 NACO Cost Survey* (s.l.: Library of Congress National Coordinated Cataloging Operations, 1987), p. 1.

3. *Ibid.*, p. 9.

4. Arlene G. Taylor, "Authority Files in Online Catalogs: an Investigation of Their Value," *Cataloging & Classification Quarterly* 4 (Spring 1984):14.

5. *Ibid.*, p. 13.

6. Catherine M. Thomas, "Authority Control in Manual Versus Online Catalogs: an Examination of "See" References," *Informational Technology and Libraries* 3, no. 4 (December 1984): 396.

7. Mark R. Watson and Arlene G. Taylor, "Implications of Current Reference Structures for Authority Work in Online Environments," *Information Technology and Libraries* 6, no. 1 (March 1987): 15.

8. *Ibid.*, p. 13.

9. *Ibid.*, p. 18.

10. Alexis J. Jamieson, Elizabeth Dolan, and Luc Declerck, "Keyword Searching vs. Authority Control in an Online Catalog," *Journal of Academic Librarianship* 12, no. 5 (November 1986); 277-283.

11. Watson and Taylor, "Implications," p. 17.

12. *Ibid.*, p. 13.

14. Watson and Taylor, "Implications," p. 17.

15. David W. Lewis, "Research on the Use of Online Catalogs and its Implications for Library Practice," *Journal of Academic Librarianship* 13, no. 3 (July 1987): 155.

APPENDIX 1

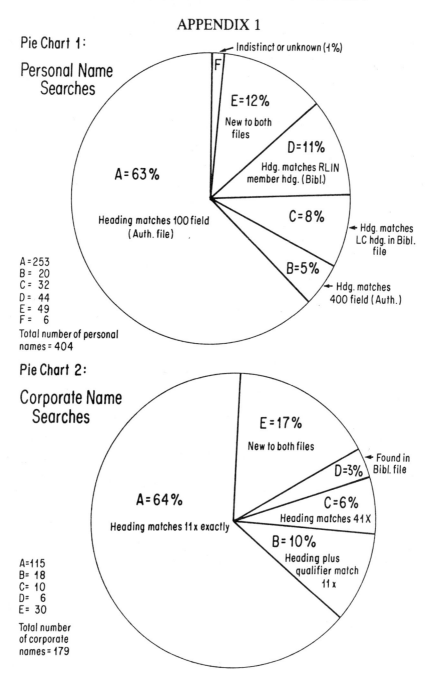

Pie Chart 1:

Personal Name
Searches

Indistinct or unknown (1%)

E=12%
New to both files

D=11%
Hdg. matches RLIN member hdg. (Bibl.)

A=63%
Heading matches 100 field (Auth. file)

C=8%
Hdg. matches LC hdg. in Bibl. file

B=5%
Hdg. matches 400 field (Auth.)

A=253
B= 20
C= 32
D= 44
E= 49
F= 6
Total number of personal names = 404

Pie Chart 2:

Corporate Name
Searches

E=17%
New to both files

D=3%
Found in Bibl. file

A=64%
Heading matches 11x exactly

C=6%
Heading matches 41X

B= 10%
Heading plus qualifier match 11 x

A=115
B= 18
C= 10
D= 6
E= 30
Total number of corporate names = 179

APPENDIX 2

Sample RLIN Bibliographic Screen

BKS/PROD   Books   MUL   Catalog   NYBY—
FIN PN WILAMOWITZ-MOELLENDORFF, U V - 154 clusters
+
1) Callimachus. [HYMNI.] CALLIMACHI HYMNI ET EPI-
GRAMMATA. Tertium edidit / (Berolini : Apud Weidmannos,
1907.)
NYBY (c-9115 NBuU)

2) DIE GRIECHISCHE UND LATEINISCHE LITERATUR UND
SPRACHE 3., stark verb. und verm. aufl. (Leipzig-Berlin, B.
G. Teubner, 1912.)
IAUG (c-9120 IaU) CASX (c-9665 CU-SB) CTYG (c-9665 CtY)
DCLC (c-9660 DLC) FLUG (c-9665 FU) NYAG (c-9665 NAIU)

3) Aeschylus. [AGAMEMNON. GERMAN] AGAMEMNON
[MICROFORM] / 3. Aufl. (Berlin : Weidmannsche Buch-
handlung, 1903.)
NYUG (c-9118 NNU *c*)

4) Sophocles. [OEDIPUS REX. GERMAN] SOPHOKLES OEDI-
PUS [MICROFORM]. 3. Aufl. (Berlin : Weidmannsche Buch-
handlung, 1903.)
NYUG (c-9118 NNU *c*) NYCG (b-9918 NNC *ccb*)

5) Sophocles. [PHILOCTETES] PHILOKTETES [MICROFORM]
/ (Berlin : Weidmannsche Buchhandlung, 1923.)
NYUG (c-9114 NNU *c*)

Variation in Personal Names in Works Represented in the Catalog

Elizabeth E. Fuller

SUMMARY. Recent research suggests that many authority records might be unnecessary in online systems with sophisticated programming. One problem in determining which names can be used without full authority records and the references they provide is that there has been little study of the names themselves, and patterns of variation are unknown. In a random sample of persons with entries in the University of Chicago library general catalog, more than 80% had names appearing in only one form in all works. The study also categorizes the differences among the forms of those names that do appear in more than one way.

INTRODUCTION

The purpose of this study is to determine the extent to which persons' names appear in different forms in their works, and, secondarily, to examine the types of differences among the forms of those names that do appear in more than one way. Variation in the way personal names are recorded or cited is one of the principal reasons authority control is needed in catalogs. Until recently catalogers dealt with these variations by recording them as references in authority records, but the search for the best way to integrate authority control functions into online library systems has encouraged a reassessment of traditional recordkeeping practices. Researchers

Elizabeth E. Fuller is Manuscript Cataloguer at the Rosenbach Museum & Library, 2010 DeLancey Place, Philadelphia, PA 19103.
This article was written as a master's paper at the University of Chicago Graduate Library School. The author wishes to thank her advisor, Arlene G. Taylor, now Associate Professor, School of Library Service, Columbia University, for overall guidance; and Judith Nadler, Head of Cataloging, and Paul M. Cairns, former Assistant to the Director, University of Chicago Library, for statistical information used in defining the sample.

make a distinction between authority records and authority control, and are beginning to investigate what functions of authority records might be better carried out by system programming.

The findings of two recent studies indicate that full authority records may be unnecessary for many names. Arlene G. Taylor, in a study of failed patron searches in Northwestern University's NOTIS system, determined that while only 6.4% of these searches would have been successful if existing authority records had been linked to the bibliographic records, 40.1% (including about half of the 6.4% above) would have been helped by programs that would either flip the search string to look for the last-input part of the name first (since many patrons enter names in direct order rather than the inverted form used in access points) or truncate the string to look for the first word and the first letter of the second word.[1] Mark R. Watson and Taylor studied name authority records and found that 68.3% of all Library of Congress machine-readable personal name authority records have no references at all, and that in a system with keyword searching and right-hand truncation capabilities, 41.5% of the references on the remaining records would be unnecessary.[2] If many authority records are thus unneeded in certain automated environments, the question of how to deal with these names in an integrated system remains. Taylor, Frost, and Maxwell, in a 1985 article, described a number of systems available through or being developed by networks and vendors.[3] Some of these systems automatically create brief authority records for names without references; some do not require authority records at all, allowing the work to be postponed until it is necessary to create references. A variety of file structures are employed for linking names with bibliographic records.

One problem in determining which names could be used without full authority records is that there has been little if any study of the names on which the records are based, and patterns of variation are unknown.[4] Melinda Shore investigated the extent to which title page forms of names differed from the forms established for use as headings.[5] However, she compared each occurrence of a name only with its established form, and her findings gave no information about how the forms found varied from each other. Even if a name was used consistently by an author, each title page occurrence that did not match the established heading was counted as a separate difference.[6] Elizabeth Tate conducted two studies of how closely the forms of names found in bibliographic citations, which are sometimes taken from title pages, matched the forms in established headings,[7] but no one has studied the names themselves.

One type of name that may not require full cataloger-created authority records in the systems Taylor and Watson envision is a name that appears in only one form in all works. The primary purpose of my study was to find out what proportion of names fall into this category. My initial estimate was that at least 75% of personal names would always appear in the same form. Among these names are those of most persons represented by a single work. William Gray Potter suggests that in most catalogs the proportion of authors who have written only one work to the total number of authors represented can be generalized to two-thirds, and that in very large catalogs the proportion conforms to Lotka's law, which predicts 60.79%.[8] It was also logical to assume that some authors of more than one work would use their names consistently. The 75% figure was based on my experience in creating authority records for the Name Authority Cooperative Project (NACO). The results of my study show that the proportion is even greater.

A second reason for undertaking this study applies as much to manual catalogs as to automated ones. Several researchers mention the question of how far a person's works would scatter in the catalog if headings were not normalized, but none has studied it.[9] Determining how much the different forms of each person's name vary from each other should give some indication of the extent of scattering, though it would be difficult to measure properly except in the context of all the other entries in a given catalog. (More important than the extent of scattering is the somewhat different question of its effect on catalog users, a question that decades of catalog use studies have not satisfactorily addressed.)

METHODOLOGY

This study required both a large collection of books that could be conveniently examined and a sampling frame that would give every person in the collection an equal chance of being selected. Potential sampling frames were automated authority or headings files, shelf-lists, and card catalogs. While authority files and shelflists were more attractive in some ways than card catalogs, they also presented several important drawbacks. All easily available automated authority or headings files contained primarily names of persons associated with works published within the last ten to fifteen years. I wanted to be able to generalize the study's findings to include a greater chronological span, because of continuing retrospective conversion, and it cannot be assumed that older and newer authors' names will exhibit the same patterns of variation. Today's authors, for example, seldom write in Latin or use pseudonyms like "Publius" or "A Gentleman of Cambridge." Many automated files contain some older personal names, but these are likely to be atypical: names of prolific authors or otherwise well-known persons whose works are still being reissued or who are the subjects of other works. A shelflist covers the same chronological period as a collection, but has two disadvantages as a sampling frame. First, while one person's works may tend to cluster together, they may also be scattered in the file, giving some persons more chance of being chosen than others if the sample is obtained by choosing random card positions. Second, since there is only one card for each item, a sample from such a file would be biased against persons whose names are not chosen as main entries.

The University of Chicago's general card catalog was chosen as the sampling frame. This catalog has limits also: it excludes some government documents, microforms, and the Far East collection, for example, but these represent only a small part of the library's holdings, and it is the most complete file the library has. Its broad chronological coverage and the collocation of all entries for each person made it the best choice.

The general catalog at the time of the study contained 7,344 numbered drawers, each 14 inches long. Most contained only 12 to 13 inches of cards; for purposes of the sample the maximum length of cards in a drawer was considered to be 13-1/2 inches. To get each person for the sample I chose a random four-digit number between 0001 and 7344 from the Rand Corporation's *A Million Random Digits* to correspond to a drawer, and a random three-digit number between 000 and 134 to correspond to a point measured in tenths of an inch from the front of the cards when they were compressed with a bar clamp to ensure even density. Because thicker cards, which have a better chance of being chosen this way, are likely to be older ones and may thus be different from the others, I used the procedure developed for an earlier study by Herman Fussler to minimize this bias, always choosing the third card after the one at the random point.[10] If the third card was not the first card for a personal name in a roman- or Cyrillic-alphabet language, I took the first such name after it. (The language restriction was due to my unfamiliarity with other alphabets and grammars, which might have caused errors in dealing with such names.) This produced some bias in favor of names following long runs of other kinds of entries, but there seems to be no reason they are likely to be different from others. It also produced a more serious bias against non-Western names. This bias must be remembered when the results are considered, since there was no practical way to include those names in this study. If the drawer contained too few cards: or no suitable ones after the chosen point, it was not used, but a new one was chosen according to the random table. If the drawer had more than 13-1/2 inches of cards, each card beyond that point was considered "linked" to one in front of the point, and if one of the linked pair had been chosen, both would have been used, though the situation did not actually occur.[11]

When a person was chosen for the sample, I determined the form of his or her name used in each work that was represented in the catalog by either a name or a name-title entry, taking the name from the catalog card if it appeared in a title page transcription or quoted note, and examining the item itself if there was no such reliable surrogate. I was able to locate all but three of the items that needed to be examined; these were all for persons for whom there was at least one recorded name usage. I recorded uses found anywhere in the item unless the person was the subject of the work, then recorded only forms that were "prominent" according to AACR2 rule 0.8.[12] When a single entry represented more than one separately published work, each work was counted separately, as if it had its own card. For example, one author card for Rida Johnson Young had only the collective title: [Plays in the Atkinson Coll.]. The call number referred to a folder containing four separate paperbound plays. They counted as four items, and her name was recorded as it appeared in each one.

The following formula furnished the minimum size for the sample:[13]

$$n = \frac{Z^2 N \; p \; (1\text{-}p)}{NE^2 + Z^2 \; p \; (1\text{-}p)}$$

where: n represents the number of items in the sample,

z represents the curve value for the confidence interval chosen (95%; curve value 1.96),

N represents the number of items in the defined universe,

p represents the proportion of items in the sample estimated to have a given attribute (here the number of persons whose names appear in more than one way, estimated to be no more than 25%, or 0.25), and

E represents the allowable error (for this study 5%).

The defined universe for this study is the number of different persons for whom there are entries in the catalog. It was determined by multiplying the estimated total number of titles in the catalog by an estimated ratio of personal name entries to titles. The figure used for the number of titles in the catalog is based on the library's measurements for the 1985 National Shelflist Count, adjusted as follows:

Total titles in shelflist at end of May 1985[14]	1,962,189
Titles added in one year[15]	40,500
Series analytics in general catalog for which there are no cards in shelflist[16]	+ 20,027
Total titles in general catalog	2,022,716
Number of personal entries per title[17]	× 1.4
Total persons represented in general catalog at end of May 1986	2,831,802

When this number is used for N in the formula above, n, the minimum sample size, is 288. The final sample consisted of 324 persons, of whom 17 appeared only as subjects.

FINDINGS

In order to see how the number of names of forms of name used by a person compares with the number of books entered under his or her name, I first counted the number of books for which the name of each person in the sample was a main or added entry, excluding subject entries to allow comparison with Potter's results. The results of the present study appear in Table 1.

Potter found that the proportion of persons represented by only one entry was 69.33% in the catalog of the University of Wisconsin-Whitewater and 63.50% at the University of Illinois at Urbana-Champaign.[18] The University of Chicago catalog, with 61.9%, approaches the proportion of single-entry persons predicted by Lotka's law even more closely.[19]

While the names of 190 persons in the sample appeared as main or added entries on only one book, many persons with two or more works consistently used their names without variation. Finding out just how many persons were so consistent was the next step in the analysis.

Determining the number of different names or forms of name* used in items entered under the heading for a person seemed at first like a simple mechanical process, but there were some unforeseen complications. If the only difference between two forms was the capitalization of a particle, was this one form or two? What if the only difference was a hyphen between the forenames? The forms certainly looked different, but under the 1980 ALA and LC filing rules, the hyphen would be treated as a space and the two forms

---

*Although some parts of the rules make a distinction between different *names* used by a person (including pseudonyms, changed names, etc.) and different *forms* of the same name, for most of this discussion the distinction is not important, and I will use the terms more or less interchangeably, preferring *forms* to cover both.

TABLE 1

Number of books per person

Number of books	Number of persons	% of persons
1	190	61.9
2	48	15.6
3	20	6.5
4	17	5.5
5	6	2.0
6	7	2.3
7	2	0.7
8	0	0.0
9	5	1.6
10	1	0.3
13	1	0.3
14	1	0.3
16	1	0.3
20	1	0.3
21	1	0.3
25	1	0.3
26	2	0.6
29	1	0.3
Total 761	307	99.9

Note: Percentages do not add up to 100.0 due to roundoff error.

would file together, so no reference would be made for one to the other in LC authority records. However, many large catalogs still use older rules that treat hyphenated forms as single words and would file them separately. Inflected names in foreign languages also caused some problems. What about a Latin name that appeared in the genitive form on a title page, when only the nominative form would be used in an authority record?

It seemed important to consider the names two ways: as they actually appeared in the works and as they would be used as authority headings or references. If the findings are to have any relevance to automated authority files, only those forms that would be used as headings or references should be counted. On the other hand, this does not give a true picture of the way names actually appear in books, and some opponents of stringent authority control have claimed that full-text searching of bibliographic records would allow names to be picked up from the title page transcription or other part of the description and eliminate the need to add authorized headings.[20] I decided therefore to make two separate counts. First I counted the number of forms that resulted when the name in each item was transcribed in accordance with AACR2 and LC Rule Interpretations. This involved few and infrequent departures from the form that actually appeared in the item. The major departures involved omission of titles of honor and address and similar terms in accordance with the provisions of rule 1.1F7; transcription of the letters i, j, u, and v according to 1.0E; and romanization according to ALA/LC tables. The second count required determining how the transcribed forms for each person would appear as headings or references on an LC/MARC name authority record (without deciding which would be chosen as the heading). Some forms disappeared in this process: "Francis De Haes Janvier" became equivalent to "Francis de Haes Janvier" since LC does not make references from differences that do not affect filing. "Martino Jugie," a Latinized name in the ablative case, became in the nominative "Martinus Jugie," but since this form was also used in one of his books, one difference disappeared. Similarly, since LC does not make references from abbreviated forms if the abbreviation always stands for the same name (RI 22.1B), "Hans v. Schubert" became the same as "Hans von Schubert."

Some names did not appear at all in the works entered under them; the catalogers had used information from other sources to determine the choice of entry for these works. Two of these persons were the subjects of works, but their names did not appear prominently in them.

Since the rules for determining choice and form of name differ for persons who have responsibility for works and those who are only the subjects of works, and the rules for making references require separate consideration of the person's own works and other sources, I decided also to tabulate the findings for both descriptive and heading or reference forms in three ways: first, including all items found for all persons in the sample; second, excluding those persons who were only the subjects of works, but including works for which persons were subject entries if the catalog also contained other kinds of entries for them; and third, excluding all subject entries. Table 2 shows the results of this analysis. Table 3 highlights the percentages of persons with single forms from Table 2 and gives the chance error and confidence intervals, or percentages in the catalog, obtained by using the sample percentages and final sample sizes in the sample size formula above.

The next part of the investigation involved categorizing the differences among the forms found for persons whose works showed more than one form, and determining the total number of forms in each category. Neither Shore's nor Watson and Taylor's categories seemed entirely appropriate for this sample. Since my concern was only with describing the forms found and not with choosing one of them to use as a heading, I decided to compare each form to the earliest form found in the person's works, or in any work for those who were only subjects. While some pairs of forms showed more than one difference, I counted only the first one found when the two names were arranged as they would be when used as access points (usually surname first) and compared from left to right. The Appendix gives examples of the types of differences included in each category. Table 4 shows the results of this evaluation.

DISCUSSION

The results show that the names of the great majority of persons represented in a large library catalog only appear in one form, and are thus unlikely to require full MARC authority records in an automated system with keyword searching and right-hand truncation capabilities. But if a person uses more than one form of his or her name, the most common point of difference between the forms is in the entry element, the most important element in a manual catalog and a difference for which an automated system could not easily substitute programming for authority records in all cases. Still, many multi-form names do exhibit differences that could be dealt with by programming, such as those in fullness or in terms associated with the names. But the number of names examined here is too small to give a statistically reliable picture of the differences. To make a meaningful comparison with Shore's or Watson and Taylor's findings, a larger sample should be taken and a heading chosen for each name on the basis of the forms found, so the others can be compared to it.

It is possible, however, to make one definite assertion about the relationship of these findings to Watson and Taylor's. If LC's current practice of making full authority records for every name in its catalog continues, the percentage of personal name records without references will increase from the 68.3% of their study. A large research library catalog more than ninety years old that is still kept current is likely to reflect the bibliographic universe more accurately than the LC authority file, which is heavily biased toward recently published materials. But as the number of machine-readable bibliographic records continues to grow through both current cataloging and retrospective conversion projects major and minor, and as the Linked Systems Project increases the proportion of these records available to individual libraries,[21] automated catalogs will become truer reflections of the bibliographic universe.

Though the percentage of referenceless records will increase, it will probably not quite reach the percentages found here for single-form persons, for two reasons. The first is that some of these names still require references under current procedures (though these may not be necessary in a more sophisticated system): multiple surnames and those with separate prefixes must have a reference from each part; initials entered in direct order must have references from inverted forms. The second reason is that pre-AACR2 headings from LC's printed records appear as references, and are often forms never used by the persons themselves. This and the fact that some names in the LC authority file are NACO contributions, for which there are not necessarily works in the LC database, mean that

TABLE 2

Number of persons represented by given number of forms

Number of forms	Descriptive transcription						Heading/reference form					
	All persons		Excluding persons appearing only as subjects		No use as subject		All persons		Excluding persons appearing only as subjects		No use as subject	
	All uses		All uses				All uses		All uses			
	#	%	#	%	#	%	#	%	#	%	#	%
0	5	1.5	3	1.0	3	1.0	5	1.5	3	1.0	3	1.0
1	264	81.5	251	81.8	253	82.4	272	84.0	258	84.0	259	84.4
2	29	9.0	28	9.1	29	9.4	26	8.0	25	8.1	26	8.5
3	11	3.4	11	3.6	10	3.3	10	3.1	10	3.3	10	3.3
4	9	2.8	8	2.6	7	2.3	6	1.9	6	2.0	4	1.3
5	1	0.3	1	0.3	0	0.0	0	0.0	0	0.0	0	0.0
6	0	0.0	0	0.0	0	0.0	0	0.0	0	0.0	0	0.0

7	1	0.3	1	0.3	2	0.7	1	0.3	1	0.3	3	1.0
8	0	0.0	0	0.0	3	1.0	1	0.3	1	0.3	2	0.7
9	1	0.3	1	0.3	0	0.0	1	0.3	1	0.3	0	0.0
10	1	0.3	1	0.3	0	0.0	2	0.6	2	0.7	0	0.0
11	2	0.6	2	0.7	0	0.0	0	0.0	0	0.0	0	0.0
Total persons	324	100.0	307	100.0	307	100.0	324	100.0	307	100.0	307	100.2
Total forms	444		425		407		422		406		394	
Avg. forms/ person	1.37		1.38		1.33		1.30		1.32		1.28	

TABLE 3

Persons with names in only one form

	% of all persons in sample	% chance error	% of persons in catalog (95% confidence interval)
Descriptive transcription			
All persons, all uses	81.5	4.1	77.1-85.4
Excluding persons appearing as subjects only	81.8	4.3	77.5-86.1
Excluding all subject uses	82.4	4.3	78.1-86.2
Heading/Reference form			
All persons, all uses	84.0	3.9	80.1-87.9
Excluding persons appearing as subjects only	84.0	3.9	80.1-87.9
Excluding all subject uses	84.4	3.9	80.5-88.3

TABLE 4

Types of differences in forms found compared to earliest form

	Descriptive transcription						Heading/reference form					
	All persons		Excluding persons appearing only as subjects				All persons		Excluding persons appearing only as subjects			
	All uses		All uses		No use as subject		All uses		All uses		No use as subject	
Type of difference	#	%	#	%	#	%	#	%	#	%	#	%
Entry element	41	32.8	40	33.1	31	30.1	35	34.0	34	33.3	29	32.2
Presence/absence of forenames	11	8.8	11	9.1	6	5.8	8	7.8	8	7.8	7	7.8
Fullness of first forename	30	24.0	30	24.8	28	27.2	27	26.2	27	26.5	25	27.8
Other difference in first forename	11	8.8	11	9.1	10	9.7	12	11.7	12	11.8	9	10.0
Other fullness	10	8.0	10	8.3	10	9.7	9	8.7	9	8.8	9	10.0
Titles and other words associated with name	16	12.8	13	10.7	12	11.7	12	11.7	12	11.8	11	12.2
Hyphens	1	0.8	1	0.8	1	1.0	0	0.0	0	0.0	0	0.0
Capitalization or diacritics	5	4.0	5	4.1	5	4.9	0	0.0	0	0.0	0	0.0
Total differences	125	100.0	121	100.0	103	100.1	103	100.1	102	100.0	90	100.0

68.3% is not a true indicator of the proportion of single-form persons in the database, but is probably an underestimate.

One limitation of this study is the exclusion of corporate names. They also need authority control, but they form a smaller proportion of the authority file and present more complex problems, and so were not included here.

Another possibility for extending this study is to include articles in periodical publications. Defining the sample population would be difficult, but such information could be useful in extending authority control to databases that integrate records for various types of materials, especially since there is growing interest in integrating periodical indexes and library catalogs. Citation indexes would certainly benefit from authority control also. It is my guess that the patterns found will be very different from those in books, since different journals have different conventions for representing authors' names and most authors probably write for more different journals than book publishers. It would also be instructive to repeat this study in libraries of different types and sizes, since public, school, and special libraries are quite different from large general research libraries and from each other in their collections and perhaps in some of the kinds of references needed by the users of their catalogs.

REFERENCES

1. Arlene G. Taylor, "Authority Files in Online Catalogs: an Investigation of Their Value," *Cataloging & Classification Quarterly* 4, no. 3 (Spring 1984): 14-15.

2. Mark R. Watson and Arlene G. Taylor, "Implications of Current Reference Structures for Authority Work in Online Environments," *Information Technology and Libraries* 6, no. 1 (Spring 1987): 13, 15.

3. Arlene G. Taylor, Margaret F. Maxwell, and Carolyn O. Frost, "Network and Vendor Authority Systems," *Library Resources and Technical Services* 29 (April/June 1985): 195-205.

4. A search of the literature shows no such studies, and William Gray Potter in "When Names Collide: Conflict in the Catalog and AACR2," *Library Resources and Technical Services* 24 (Winter 1980): 3-16, said that he had found none.

5. Melinda L. Shore, "Variation Between Personal Name Headings and Title Page Usage," *Cataloging & Classification Quarterly* 4, no. 4 (Summer 1984): 1-11.

6. Ibid., 5.

7. Elizabeth L. Tate, "Main Entries and Citations: One Test of the Revised Cataloging Code," *Library Quarterly* 33 (1963): 172-91; "Access Points and Citations: a Comparison of Four Cataloging Codes," *Library Research* 1 (1979): 347-59.

8. Potter, "When Names Collide," 8-9.

9. Shore, "Variation," 1; Potter, "When Names Collide," 4, 10; Åke I. Koel, "Bibliographic Control at the Crossroads: Do We Get Our Money's Worth?" *Journal of Academic Librarianship* 7 (1981): 222.

10. The derivation of this formula is explained in Abraham Bookstein, "Sampling From Card Files," *Library Quarterly* 53 (Fall 1983): 310-11.

11. Ibid., 308-309, for further explanation of linking.

12. "The word *prominently* . . . means that a statement to which it applies must be a formal statement found in one of the prescribed sources of information . . . for areas 1 and 2 [the title and statement of responsibility area and the edition area] for the class of material to which the item being catalogued belongs." *Anglo-American Cataloguing Rules*, 2nd ed., edited by Michael Gorman and Paul W. Winkler. Chicago: American Library Association, 1978, p. 3.

13. Formula from Cecil H. Meyers, *Elementary Business and Economic Statistics*, 2nd ed. (Belmont, Calif.: Wadsworth Pub. Co., 1970), 292. Quoted in Arlene Taylor Dowell, *AACR 2 Headings: A Five-Year Projection of Their Impact on Catalogs* (Littleton, Colo.: Libraries Unlimited, 1982), 36.

14. Estimated, using a ratio of 3.84 titles/mm, by Paul M. Cairns, Assistant to the Director, University of Chicago Library. Memo dated 6 December 1985.

15. Approximate growth of collection in both FY83/84 and FY84/85, from statistical supplement to *Annual Report* of Assistant Director for Technical Services, University of Chicago Library, 1985. Cited by Paul M. Cairns, personal communication, 25 April 1986.

16. Estimated at 1% of total number of titles in shelflist by Judith Nadler, Head, Cataloging Department, University of Chicago Library, personal communication, April 1986.

17. Based on a ratio of 1289 personal name headings to 926 records in a sample from a large library catalog in Dowell, *AACR 2 Headings*, 43, 48.

18. Potter, "When Names Collide," 6-7.

19. It is not possible to conclude from this alone, however, that the catalog conforms to Lotka's distribution. That would require statistically significant data about number of persons represented by more than one item, since the distribution predicts the proportion of authors who write any given number of works. This sample was too small to provide such data.

20. Frederick G. Kilgour, "Design of Online Catalogs," in *The Nature and*

Future of the Catalog: Proceedings of the ALA's Information Science and Auto-mation Division's 1975 and 1977 Institutes on the Catalog, ed. Maurice J. Freed-man and S. Michael Malinconico (Phoenix: Oryx Press, 1979), 40; Hugh C. Atkinson, "The Electronic Catalog," in same volume, 103.

21. For a description and short history of this project, see Henriette D. Avram, "The Linked Systems Project: Its Implications for Resource Sharing," *Library Resources and Technical Services* 30 (January/March 1986): 36-46.

APPENDIX

Examples of names or forms in Table 4 categories

Entry element

This category includes, but is not limited to, pseudonyms, changes of name for marriage or other reasons, abbreviation of sur-name, and differences of romanization, language, or spelling. The names involved may be surnames, forenames, or a combination.

Madame de Charriere
Zelide

Muriel Wheldale
Muriel Wheldale Onslow

Mary E. Blake
M. E. B.

Aurel Vijoli
Aurel Vizholi

Afonso Dalboquerque
Afonso de Albuquerque

Charitonos Aphrodisieos
Chariton of Aphrodisios

E. Ysbrants Ides
Everard Isbrand

Some of these differences are due to grammatical endings and appear only in descriptive transcription, since the nominative form matches the entry word of the other form. In the heading form, however, there may be another type of difference.

Austen Henry Layard
Henry Layardin (Turkish possessive form)
Henry Layard (Nominative form)

Presence/absence of forenames

It seemed advisable to separate these differences from the category of first forename fullness since truncation programs would have to handle them differently. This category includes pairs of names in which one has one or more forenames and the other has none; it may or may not have a title or other words attached.

Francis Carco
Carco

Dr. Capitan
L. Capitan

Joseph E. Portlock
Major-Gen. Portlock

Fullness of first forename

Includes pairs in which the first name is fuller than the second and those in which it is less full.

M. Jugie
Martin Jugie

Iv. Khadzhov
Ivan Khadzhov

Vanna Gazzola Stachini
V. Gazzola Stachini

Other differences in first forename

Does not include pairs in which one or both forenames are points of entry; these are included in the entry element category.

Soume Tcheng
Soumay Tcheng

Bernardus Maria Ignatius Delfgaauw
Bernard Delfgaauw

Austen Henry Layard
Henry Austen Layard

Other fullness

Includes fullness or presence/absence of second or later fore-names and of particles which are part of the surname.

Frances Ann Shirley
Frances A. Shirley

Patrick D. Trevor-Roper
Patrick Trevor-Roper

Hans von Schubert
Hans v. Schubert (Descriptive difference only; no reference)

Giovanni Pierluigi da Palestrina
Giovanni Pierluigi Palestrina

Titles and other words associated with name

This category includes names showing differences in terms that are included in MARC subfield c. In determining which differences are encountered first in left-to-right order, I have followed LC practice in placing all such terms after the forenames, rather than placing some, like "Mrs." and "Sir," in front, as AACR2 prescribes. Since LC considers headings in this form to be AACR2 and uses the form on its MARC records, and many libraries accept them this way, the results will be more meaningful if this tabulation follows LC practice. Thus the pair

Mrs. Kenneth F. Rich
Adena Miller Rich

is counted with other differences in first forename since the LC form of the first is "Rich, Kenneth F., Mrs."

Names in this category differ from the earliest form found in the presence or absence of such terms or in the form or content of the terms themselves.

Lyon Playfair
Sir Lyon Playfair

Madame de Charriere
Frau von Charriere

Hno. Nectario Maria
hermano Nectario Maria

Vincentus Burgundius
Vincentus Bellovasensis

Some differences disappear when the names are put in heading form:

mm. Hartmann . . .
Messrs Hartmann . . . Both become "Hartmann, M."

Hyphens

See discussion in text.

P.-A. Dufau
P. A. Dufau

Capitalization and diacritics only

Catalogers are supposed to supply diacritical marks that are missing from an item if the language requires them (AACR2 1.0G), but this is difficult to do for some names at the descriptive stage when there may be no other information about the name available. The same is true of capitalization of particles in names; at the descriptive stage the person's preference (the guide prescribed by rule A.13B) may not be known. Hence, names that differ only in these respects count only in the descriptive transcription, since references are not made from such forms.

Gérard de Catalogne
Gerard de Catalogne

Francis de Haes Janvier
Francis De Haes Janvier

Uniform Titles for Music:
An Exercise in Collocating Works

Richard P. Smiraglia

SUMMARY. The uniform title is viewed historically as an artificial device to collocate works. In music cataloging, problems of multiple manifestations with variant title pages lead to the development of uniform titles that would both collocate and distinguish, and ultimately serve as identifiers for musical works. A principal problem in the authority control of works is recognition of multiple manifestations and the concomitant syndetic depth. Research suggests a low incidence of multiple manifestations among textual works, but hints that a greater incidence might be found among musical works. An empirical study is conducted using a sample of musical works and locating for each all physical manifestations in OCLC and the NUC. Virtually the entire sample of musical works yielded multiple manifestations. A majority of the manifestations had titles proper different from that of the first edition of the work. It is concluded that an authority-controlled collocating device is necessary for musical works, that more references are required, and that links among authority records for works could provide increased syndetic depth.

INTRODUCTION

The Uniform Title

The uniform title has always been a device used to collocate works, and in its earliest incarnations was often confused with subject headings. We are told that even Callimachus used form headings to gather related works together,[1] but it is usually Panizzi's use

Richard P. Smiraglia is Senior Lecturer, School of Library Service, Columbia University, New York, NY 10027.

This research was conducted with the assistance of a grant from the Research Board of the University of Illinois at Urbana-Champaign. The author also wishes to acknowledge the assistance of Dean Jensen, Char Kneevers, and Robert Cianchette.

97

of form headings (such as "Academies," "Ephemerides," "Dictionaries," Liturgies," etc., as well as the ubiquitous "Bible" heading that is still with us) for works that were anonymous or works of mixed responsibility that is cited as the first use of what are now called uniform titles.[2] Works of personal authorship have been collocated under what have come to be known as conventional titles since Cutter, who prescribed this treatment for classical works that existed in multiple manifestations.[3] Categorical filing arrangements have also been used to subarrange variant manifestations of works by a personal author and it was a short step from this practice to the practice of writing the filing element on the card. Eventually rules were adopted for the choice and form of the conventional titles.[4] Uniform titles that differentiate among works with similar characteristics have been used for musical works for most of this century, but this practice has only recently been recognized by a 1985 revision to the *Anglo-American Cataloguing Rules*, second edition *(AACR2)*.[5] This provision was used to extend the dual collocating and distinguishing functions of uniform titles to serial publications.

Obviously the uniform title serves a variety of functions simultaneously. The uniform title identifies the particular intellectual entity (Homer's *Iliad*, for instance). It collocates the manifestations of the work that have appeared under differing titles proper (Dickens' *Sketches by Boz* and *Esquisses de Boz*, for example, will be found in one place). It distinguishes among works that have similar bibliographic characteristics and would therefore be indistinguishable in the catalogue without an artificial device (for example, serials titled *Bulletin* would be indistinguishable without the addition of the names of the corporate bodies responsible for them). Other additions to uniform titles, including most notably the names of languages of translations, serve to help the user reduce recall in a search by retrieving only headings for works that will ultimately be useful.

Music Uniform Titles

The history of music cataloging is essentially the story of the search for solutions to the problems of identifying, collocating and distinguishing musical works. Problems of multiple manifestations with variant title pages were endemic in music libraries. It was always unlikely that the bibliographic approach to descriptive cataloging advocated by Panizzi and his successors would achieve a unique entry for a given musical item, because it was unlikely that the mere juxtaposition of a name heading for a composer over the transcribed title proper would constitute an adequate heading for the work.

Some early (mostly European) approaches utilized systematic transcription of the elements that would both properly identify the work and create order in composer files. Anglo-American catalogers had already discovered the usefulness of collocating works with "descriptive" titles (what we now term "distinctive") under the original title, and had begun to present it in square brackets preceding the title page title, so as to ensure the creation of a proper heading given the juxtaposition of the composer's name. For works with titles that utilized musical terminology (sonatas and so forth) elements were to be transposed to achieve useful entries, with elements such as key and opus number added in square brackets if they were absent from the title page.

Codification of these practices occurred gradually due in part to the joint work of the Music Library Association and the American Library Association and the eventual incorporation of various draft provisions into codes from 1949 to the present. In these codes a distinct differentiation occurs between the two types of musical titles. Works with distinctive titles are treated much like textual works and are collocated under an original title, with additions used to indicate translation, alternative accompaniment, or other alterations to the musical manifestation. Other works are collocated under the name of type of composition, with additions made according to reasonably inflexible provisions for medium of performance, serial, opus and thematic index number, and key. These uniform titles, usually referred to with the misnomer "generic," are the successor of the conventional titles of the 1940s. In either case, the use of these uniform titles is widespread, and the codification and regular revision of the provisions for them in mainstream textual cataloging codes is a reflection of the recognition that musical works not only appear in multiple manifestations but are collected that way as well.[6]

Authority Control for Works

As Arlene G. Taylor points out elsewhere in this issue, authority control of works has only recently begun to receive the attention of researchers. A principle problem is the recognition of multiple manifestations of works in the bibliographic universe (as well as the individual library catalog), and the complexity of the connections that must be made among them and between their descriptions and the uniform heading made for the work. Bregzis' discussion of syndetic structures notes a gradual shift from Cutter's record-syndetic structure to what he terms an entry-syndetic structure. Bregzis points out that though the entry-syndetic "method was neat and mechanically efficient . . . it narrowed the variety and contextual flexibility of catalog record correlation."[7] What Bregzis called the record syndetic structure, references that lead always to the complete bibliographic representation of a work, was discarded when unit-record systems were introduced, in favor of an entry syndetic structure, which is focused on the syndetics of the name heading. Bregzis also notes that syndetic depth, or the extent and variety of syndetic relationships, "cannot be expected to be increased through the automation of the entry syndetic structure."[8]

But music catalogs have never completely abandoned the record-syndetic structure because of their reliance on the uniform title as the heading for a work. Thus, syndetic structures in music catalogs have always contained the increased complexity of the references required within a composer's file to lead to the appropriate heading for a given musical work. Despite the decades of work on formulating rules for the creation of these headings there has been no research conducted in this area. In 1985 Smiraglia, discussing the controversy over choice of basic uniform titles for musical works noted that "There is no consistency of thought in this area and there is also no research to inform such thought. As a result, there can be no theoretical formulation that can apply."[9] Nevertheless, it seems likely that the syndetic depth of a catalog of musical works would be greater than that of a general library catalog.

Also in 1985, McNellis undertook a study of multiple and varying physical manifestations of textual works. Using a sample of works drawn from the Regenstein Library at the University of Chicago she found that approximately 26% of the works existed in multiple physical manifestations. Among other things, she concluded that "in cataloging, uniform titles may not be necessary very often for distinguishing physical manifestations," though she concedes that in both pre-order searching and in interlibrary loan "there might be considerable trouble distinguishing desired manifestations."[10]

The only indication that real differences might exist between catalogs of book collections and catalogs of music collections was presented by Papakhian in 1985. Replicating studies of the frequency of name-heading occurrence in general library catalogs, Papakhian found a percentage similar to previous studies (61.23%) in the music and books catalog at Indiana University's Music Library. This was consistent with earlier findings that "between 60 and 69 percent of all authors produce only one work."[11] However, Papakhian found that in the sound recordings catalog only 47.64 percent of personal name headings occurred only once, indicating "alterations in catalog structure may result from the inclusion of recordings or other nontraditional library formats in integrated catalogs."[12] Among the factors Papakhian notes that might have influenced this outcome is the recognition that "sound recording collections would contain . . . numerous recordings of the same work."[13] Given Papakhian's finding it seems likely that McNellis's figures for multiple manifestations of textual works might be considerably lower than that for musical works.

THE STUDY

This project was designed to look at some of the problems inherent in collocation of musical works. Areas for examination are:

1. Do musical works exist in multiple physical manifestations?

Every music librarian is aware of the variety of multiple manifestations that may exist for any given musical work. It would be interesting to note whether there is any relationship between the percentage of works with multiple manifestations and the percentages McNellis found in the general library collection. Further, it would be interesting to discover whether differences were greater with printed music or sound recordings.

2. How much do titles proper of musical works differ from edition to edition?

That is, to what extent are we certain that a collocation problem really exists? Is it true that musical works appear regularly under a variety of titles proper? If differences among variant titles proper are minimal it might be possible to formulate a simpler basic rule that would require little or no reference work and thus little or no authority control, thus reducing professional costs dramatically. On the other hand, if differences are consistently great then it would seem that the expense of formulating and maintaining uniform titles is justified.

3. Among the various titles proper that appear on editions of musical works, is one identifiable as the most common, and if so, can a pattern among different works be observed?

Given evidence of substantial difference among titles proper for the same edition, it would be useful to know whether one title or one type of title was more common than others. If so, it would be useful to know further whether a pattern could be observed among various musical works. If such patterns were consistently verifiable it could be less expensive always to use as the uniform title that title proper that fits the pattern.

4. Can the observed differences among titles proper be associated with historical trends in the music and music publishing industries?

In an earlier study Van Fossan noted a marked difference between titles proper of printed music and those of the same works on sound recordings. She noted also that "fewer recording companies are responsible for the greater numbers of recordings, and more music publishers are responsible for the proportionally smaller number of scores."[14] Can a point of diminishing returns be associated with historical trends such that it can be defined as a function of change over time?

Questions

Specifically, the questions under investigation are:

1. For a given musical work, do multiple manifestations exist in the bibliographic universe?
2. Among the manifestations of a given musical work, what percentage of all titles proper are different from that of the first edition?
3. Of those titles proper that differ from that of the first edition:
   (a) what percentage difference is attributable to variant languages?
   (b) what percentage difference is attributable to the use of entirely different titles?
4. Can a pattern be observed among the titles proper that recur with the greatest frequency?

The Sample

A sample of musical works was constructed. Then, for each work, bibliographic records representing all physical manifestations were located in the printed catalogs of the Library of Congress and in the online union catalog of OCLC. The simple random sample of musical works was drawn from the second edition of *A Basic Music Library*. . . .[15] A basic list was chosen, rather than the catalog of a particular library because we have no reliable information about the ways in which various collections of music materials may be similar. Results of a sample drawn from a particular library's catalog could be generalized to the catalogs of other collections only with considerable difficulty. To the extent that the musical works listed in *A Basic Music Library* are representative of a core collection of musical works, it should be possible to generalize results to the core collection at large and thus make statements that will be meaningful for all collections that include this essential core. To the extent that the "essential core" is representative of the *kinds* of musical works *cataloged* by libraries, and there is some evidence of this,[16] it should be possible to generalize from this sample to the larger universe of musical works in general.

A Basic Music Library contains entries for 1711 musical works numbered consecutively through five categories: score anthologies, study scores, performing editions, vocal scores, and instrumental methods. The only instrumental categories not included are guitar and recorder music. Since instrumental music could be said to form a homogenous group in terms of the ways in which titles proper are formulated (for example, it is commonplace for composers to use the name of the type of composition and terms indicating the medium of performance in the formulation of titles referred to as "generic") this limitation is not considered serious. That is, there is nothing remarkable about the guitar or recorder literature that would be likely to influence the outcome of this study.

Van Fossan's preliminary work suggested an association between the amount of variation observed among titles proper for a work and the kind of title proper. Consequently it was considered desirable to attempt stratification by type of title proper. Post-stratification was used because the structure of the sampling frame did not easily permit such strata to be drawn independently without reordering the list.

Two strata were drawn, one consisting of works with titles that are distinctive, the other of those that are not (hereafter, "generic"). The homogeneity of each of these groups is suggested by the rules in *AACR2* that prescribe different treatment for the two types of title. A narrow definition of "work" was used. For example, a vocal score was considered to be different from the full score of a work. There were 154 musical works in the combined strata. There were 79 works assigned to the "generic titles" stratum and 75 works assigned to the "distinctive titles" stratum. These strata were designed to be of sufficient size to make statements with 85% certainty that the proportions found are within ±8% of the true proportions. The low confidence level was used for two reasons. First, because the purpose of this study was to identify proportional trends, greater precision was not considered to be of crucial importance. The second reason, of course, was to facilitate the study. Given the potential number of variant titles proper per work, a larger sample size could easily have proven unmanageable. The *National Union Catalog: Music, Books on Music, and Sound Recordings* and its predecessors from 1953-1983 yielded 1632 bibliographic records for manifestations of the 154 works. Likewise, 2951 bibliographic records were located in the OCLC Online Union Catalog prior to September 1984. All duplicate OCLC records were eliminated from the sample.

In the process of comparing records from the two sources it was necessary to check for overlap to eliminate the possibility of duplication. The overlap between the sources was substantial but not complete. Examination of the records indicated that 15.4% of the NUC copy was for scores, and 84.6% was for recordings. This ratio was consistent from cumulation to cumulation. Ultimately 50.6% of the NUC records were located in OCLC (51% of the scores and 50.5% of the recordings). Most were OCLC member-input LC records, since this study occurred prior to the LC implementation of the MARC music format. Of the records found in the NUC only 4.6% were contributed by libraries other than LC. There was no evidence that records for materials produced by any particular publisher or manufacturer or even any identifiable grouping of publishers or manufacturers were more likely to appear in OCLC. Likewise, although most records carried dates of publication between 1953 and 1978 (corresponding to the years of the NUC volumes searched), no pattern emerged to suggest a relationship between date of publication and likelihood of inclusion in OCLC.

It is interesting to note that although approximately half of the NUC records were located in OCLC, these represented only 20% of the total number of the physical manifestations identified in the study. Thus a very large number (potentially nearly 80%) of the potential referents (titles proper that differ in some way from the derived, authority controlled uniform title) cannot be expected to occur in LC name authority records because the variants will not come to the attention of LC's catalogers. However, analysis suggests that LC does have those manifestations that carry the most commonly used titles proper for most works. This would indicate that at least the most commonly used variants would be available to LC catalogers. If they are used as references, then those who rely on the LC Name Authority File for authority control will have the most common cases covered to the extent that their collections coincide with or are narrower than that of the Library of Congress.

Results

Some indications of central tendency describing the musical works are indicated in Table 1. Virtually the entire sample (87.3% in the distinctive stratum and 89.8% in the generic stratum) yielded multiple manifestations. Works with distinctive titles averaged 15 manifestations that carried 3 different titles proper. Works with generic titles averaged 35 manifestations on which 11 different titles proper were found.

Having shown a distinct pattern of multiple manifestations the next step was to discover the percentage of all titles proper that differed from the title of the first physical manifestation (i.e., edition, recording, etc.; hereinafter referred to as "edition") of the work. For each work in the two strata the title proper of the first edition was ascertained using standard musicological reference tools. Variation was great, as had been expected, with the titles of the works in the distinctive stratum varying from the original 23.9% of the time and those in the generic title stratum varying 68.6% of the time.

The binomial proportion confidence interval was calculated for these percentages to ascertain the proximity of the percentages found in this study to the actual percentages existing in the population. These calculations performed at the 85% confidence level yielded ±6% for the distinctive title stratum proportion and ±14% for the proportion in the generic title stratum. The wide interval is obviously the result of the standard error used to calculate the sample size, but it does not alter the trend indicated, which is that there is little variation among the titles of manifestations of works with distinctive titles and great variation among the titles of manifestations of works with generic titles.

The material-specific differences within the strata are also interesting. That is, there tended to be fewer scores than recordings in each stratum and there tended to be greater variation in the titles on the recordings than on the scores.

The titles proper that were different from the original title of the

Table 1: Manifestations, Titles, and Variation

	Works	Mean Number of Manifestations Per Work	Mean Number of Titles Per Work	% of Titles Varying From 1st Ed.
Distinctive				
Total	71*	15.4	3	23.9
Scores	70	6.5	3	21.2
Recordings	29	22	5.5	47
Generic				
Total	79	35.1	11	68.6
Scores	77	8.9	1.3	65.2
Recordings	54	38.7	2	81.5

*No manifestations were located for four works.

work were examined to see if a trend could be observed. Table 2 illustrates the variation that can be attributed to translation. As had been expected there was a wide variation in the languages among the recorded titles proper. One hundred forty-eight of the works (95%) exhibited differences due to language variation.

Selections from the titles found for two examples illustrate the kind of variation that is common among musical works. The first, Brahms' *Academic Festival Overture* (Figure 1), is from the distinctive title stratum. The most heavily used title on recordings was *Academic Festival Overture* while the most common on scores is *Akademische Fest-Overture*. The second example, Beethoven's fifth piano concerto (Figure 2), is from the non-distinctive title stratum. The most common title on the recordings is *Piano concerto no. 5 in E-flat major, op. 73, Emperor Concerto*. There was too much variation to declare any title proper most common on scores, though German language titles clearly predominate. These cases are

Table 2: Language Variation

	Distinctive	Generic
English	57	65
French	9	8
German	16	20
Italian	8	1
Spanish	3	0
Other	4	4

*Percentage of Difference due to Language.

Figure 1: Brahms' Academic Festival

	Occurrence		
	Scores	Recordings	Total
Academic festival overture	3	32	35
Akademische Fest-Ouverture	7	6	13
Ouverture per una festa academica	1	0	1

Figure 2: Beethoven's Emperor Concerto

	Scores	Occurrence Recordings	Total
Piano concerto no. 5 in E-flat major op. 73, Emperor Concerto	0	35	35
Concerto no. 5 in E-flat major, op. 73, Emperor	1	13	14
Konzert Nr. 5, fur Klavier und Orchester, Opus 73	1	0	1
Konzert Es-dur fur Klavier und Orchester, Op. 73	1	0	1
Funftes Concert, Opus 73 in Es	1	0	1

typical in that the scores tend to reflect the original title in its original language, but the recordings tend to reflect a common English-language title.

In an attempt to discover any variation that might be associated with the age of a work, the works were grouped by date of composition into broad periods, and the number of manifestations and the percentage of variation in the titles proper were calculated. These figures are shown in Table 3. It had seemed logical that less variation might be experienced with newer works, and the chronological distribution seems to indicate such a trend. In fact, it was frequently observed during the tabulation. Great variation seemed to exist among the titles on the manifestations of popular eighteenth and nineteenth century works, but twentieth century works showed surprisingly little variation. Figure 3 shows the titles that occurred on manifestations of *Barber's Adagio for strings*.

The binomial proportion confidence intervals for all sub-strata were too large to consider the specific proportions statistically significant. Although this indicates the relative unreliability of the specific proportions, the trends observed are logical and could be more precisely verified with a sample designed accordingly.

Distinct differences were observed between the works in the two strata. For example, works with distinctive titles, such as Bach's *English Suites*, tend to vary mostly by translation into a different

Table 3: Manifestations, and Variation by Period*

	Distinctive		Generic	
	Mean No. of Manifestations Per Work	Percentage Variation	Mean No. of Manifestations Per Work	Percentage Variation
1600–1750	24	52.25	15	70.1
1750–1850	26	38.8	73	89
1850–1900	18.9	24.8	69.8	94.6
1900–	15.5	22.5	28.4	52.2

*Discrepancies with the figures in Table 1 are due to the assignment of works to periods

language, and this tendency is most pronounced on sound recordings (Figure 4). These changes seem to indicate a certain bibliographic stability that is gained when a composer assigns a specific, distinctive title to a work. Another common distinctive title variation also illustrated by Figure 4 is the technique of surrounding the original title with other terms. One result of this kind of variation is an increase in the effectiveness of keyword searching. Notice that in Figure 4, a majority of the manifestations utilize the original title *Englische Suiten*.

On the other hand, the works in the generic title stratum were very much alike. That is, like the Beethoven example in Figure 2, the same elements tended always to be present (albeit sometimes

Figure 3: Barber's Adagio

	Occurrence		
	Scores	Recordings	Total
Adagio for strings, op. 11	3	12	15
Adagio for strings	6	12	18
Adagio for string orchestra	0	3	3

Figure 4: Bach's English Suites

	Occurrence		
	Scores	Recordings	Total
Englische Suiten	12	6	18
English Suites	0	5	5
6 English Suites	2	2	4
6 Englische Suiten	1	1	2
Sechs Englische Suiten	3	1	4
Sechs grosse Suiten, genannt Englische Suiten	1	1	2
Angliiske Siuity	2	0	2

translated) but a variety of permutations was possible. In this stratum the only bibliographic stability observed was the tendency for recordings to cluster around a particular title. This might result from the tendency of a single record company to use one title for a given work on all of the manifestations it produces. More detailed discographical study could verify this practice.

CONCLUSIONS

The large confidence intervals mean that few specific quantitative conclusions can be drawn from this study, but certain trends are clearly indicated. First, it is apparent that an authority controlled collocating device is necessary to satisfy the collocating function for musical works. While the range of variation among titles proper on manifestations of musical works varies, the very fact of its existence is enough to make this point. The importance of the music uniform title, however, goes beyond its collocating function, which could be easily accomplished by merely linking bibliographic records. The distinguishing feature of the music uniform title is its ability to serve simultaneously to collocate manifestations of a work as well as to distinguish among and organize logically works in a given type of composition. In the future electronic catalog designed along the lines of those projected by Gorman and others,[17] links among authority records for *works* and the corresponding bibliographic records for their physical manifestations, as well as potential links among authority records themselves for works displaying characteristics of certain bibliographic relationships, will provide the increased syndetic depth called for by Bregzis.

Related to the success of the current entry-syndetic structure is the finding that the amount of variation observed among titles for works in the non-distinctive category would seem to indicate a need for more references to be made in authority records. The Library of Congress cannot be expected to supply all of the additional references since, obviously, the scope of their collection is narrower than that of the "national" collection. It seems likely that the increasing scope of the NACO project for music libraries will help to alleviate this problem.

Perhaps the most significant conclusion that can be drawn from this study is the evidence of the existence of multiple manifestations of a broad category of works, and the indication of great variety in bibliographic presentation. Further, it is interesting to speculate on the extent to which the patterns observed here might also be observed among other kinds of works. In particular, it seems likely that the pattern observed in the distinctive title stratum might recur on other, non-musical, dramatic works.

NOTES

1. Strout, Ruth French. "The Development of the Catalog and Cataloging Codes." In *Reader in Classification and Descriptive Cataloging*, edited by Ann F. Painter. Washington: NCR Microcard Editions, 1972, p. 161.

2. British Museum. "Rules for the Compilation of the Catalogue." In *The Catalogue of Printed Books in the British Museum*. London, 1841, vol. 1: v-ix. See particularly rules LXXIX-XC.

3. Cutter, Charles A. *Rules for a Dictionary Catalogue*. 4th ed., rewritten. Washington, DC: GPO, 1904. See particularly rules 144, 147, and 331.

4. Spalding, C. Sumner, "Music Authority Files at the Library of Congress." *Music Cataloging Bulletin* 10 (Oct. 1979): 4-6.

5. "Revisions 1985." In *Anglo-American Cataloguing Rules*. 2nd ed. Chicago: American Library Association, 1985. See rule 25.2A, paragraph 3.

6. For a more detailed history of these developments see Smiraglia, Richard P. "Chapter 2: Descriptive Cataloging." In *Music Cataloging*. In press. Philadelphia, 1987, pp. 12-47.

7. Bregzis, Ritvars. "The Syndetic Structure of the Catalog." In *Authority Control: The Key to Tomorrow's Catalog*. Edited by Mary W. Ghikas. Phoenix: Oryx Press, 1982, p. 22.

8. Bregzis, "Syndetic Structure," p. 23.

9. Smiraglia, Richard P. "Theoretical Considerations in the Bibliographic Control of Music Materials in Libraries." *Cataloging & Classification Quarterly* 5 (1985): 11.

10. McNellis, Claudia Houk. "Describing Reproductions: Multiple Physical Manifestations in the Bibliographical Universe." *Cataloging & Classification Quarterly* 5 (1985): 47.

11. Potter, William Gray. "When Names Collide: Conflict in the Catalog and AACR2." *Library Resources & Technical Services* 24 (1980): 9.

12. Papakhian, Arsen R. "The Frequency of Personal Name Headings in the Indiana University Music Library Card Catalogs." *Library Resources & Technical Services* 29 (1985): 285.

13. Papakhian, Arsen R. "Frequency," 284.

14. Van Fossan, Katherine. "The Use of Uniform Titles with Musical Materials: A Preliminary Study." Typescript. Urbana, IL, 1983, p. 27.

15. *A Basic Music Library: Essential Scores and Books.* 2nd ed. compiled by the Music Library Association Committee on Basic Music Collection under the direction of Pauline S. Bayne; edited by Robert Michael Fling. Chicago: American Library Association, 1983.

16. Smiraglia and Papakhian searched the citations in the first edition of *A Basic Music Library* in OCLC and found bibliographic records for 91.5% of the scores in the list, indicating they were held by member libraries. See Smiraglia, Richard P. and Papakhian, Arsen R. "Music in the OCLC Online Union Catalog: A Review." *Notes* 38 (1981): 267-274.

17. Gorman, Michael, "Authority Control in the Prospective Catalog." In *Authority Control: The Key to Tomorrow's Catalog.* Edited by Mary W. Ghikas. Phoenix: Oryx Press, 1982, pp. 166-180.

Authority Control in NOTIS

Roberta F. Kirby

SUMMARY. The NOTIS Authority Control Module is based on the MARC Format for Authorities. Because NOTIS is an integrated system, the functions of online create/edit, security, and indexing for authority records is very similar to that for bibliographic records. NOTIS also offers a great deal of flexibility in workflow for authority control.

INTRODUCTION

The foundation of the NOTIS authority control module is the *MARC Formats for Bibliographic Data* and the *MARC Format for Authorities*. It is through use of the structure and values in these MARC formats that authority control operates. In addition, NOTIS has defined a number of supplementary MARC-type values for authority records to permit the representation of authority data in a local system as opposed to a national utility.

The advantage of using USMARC formats for bibliographic and authority records is the flexibility of data transfer between outside vendors and a local NOTIS system. This may take the form of receiving bibliographic and/or authority records from a vendor, such as the LCSH-MARC tapes, or of sending bibliographic and/or authority records to a utility, such as RLIN. NOTIS also provides the capability to download authority and bibliographic records from the bibliographic utilities online.

Roberta F. Kirby is a systems analyst with NOTIS Systems, Inc., 1007 Church Street, Evanston, IL 60201-3622.

ONLINE RECORD VALIDATION

The most obvious feature of the NOTIS authority control module is the online create/edit function. When staff members create or edit bibliographic and authority records, the system validates the tags, indicators, subfields, and fixed field values online. Very specific error messages indicate the nature of any input errors. Furthermore, the create/edit functions for bibliographic and authority records are the same, which facilitates the training of library staff who need to work with both types of records. In addition, the system generates, upon request, double spaced worksheets for both bibliographic and authority records, that can be used for off-line editing and quality control.

TECHNICAL PROCESSING WORKFLOW

The features of the NOTIS authority control module permit a great deal of flexibility in structuring the workflow within a technical services work area. The various authority control tasks can be handled either pre- or post-production, depending on the needs of the organization.

This flexibility is provided through the generation of a number of batch products related to bibliographic and authority control activities in the online system. The report of name headings new to the database, as well as the report for name headings that have been dropped from the database can be used to accomplish post-production name authority control. The report for new and dropped subject headings can be used in a similar fashion. These reports are produced for each technical services unit so that within a NOTIS installation, there can be further flexibility across the various technical services units.

If a pre-production authority workflow is needed, this is facilitated by online indexing and searching of both bibliographic and authority records. Access can also be provided to both name and subject authority resource files maintained in the local system.

Another important issue in arranging technical services workflow is the integrity of the authority file. To have consistent heading usage in all bibliographic records from various technical services work areas in the same system, the decision may be made to have one authority record for an established heading. NOTIS provides the capability to establish an authority record as *the* authority record, allowing various technical services units to search and display the record, but restricting update access to specific staff members.

An installation also can make its own decisions as to the extent of authority control maintained over the bibliographic database. In NOTIS, an authority record is not required for every established heading. Rather, authority records are created only when cross-references or information notes are needed. However, an installation may choose to have an authority record for every established heading. The installation may also choose to selectively perform full authority control, for example, for name headings and subject headings but not for series headings.

GLOBAL HEADING CHANGES

Even if a NOTIS installation has had their bibliographic database "massaged" by a vendor both to correspond to AACR2 forms of headings and to insure consistent heading usage, there will be a need to have heading change capability on an ongoing basis. NOTIS provides this through a series of global heading change programs.

The most convenient of these makes use of the MARC authority record to change the headings in the bibliographic file. This process is a one-to-one replacement, an older or variant form (4XX) for the established heading (1XX). This process is operator initiated by a command issued when displaying the authority record. These requests for global heading changes are processed in a batch mode, utilizing the indexes to the bibliographic records to locate possible matching headings. A series of reports generated from this global heading change process notifies the staff of the records that were changed, and of the authority records used to make those changes.

The other two methods of global heading changes, while requiring more programmer intervention, offer special capabilities. For example, any subdivision in a subject heading field can be accessed and replaced. Thus, one could request that the program scan the database to identify and replace the older forms of the subject heading geographic subdivision "New York."

It can also perform subfield specific replacement in corporate name headings, such as "University of California" for "California. University." without affecting the remaining subfields. Once again, a series of reports notifies the staff of the records that were changed by these processes.

SECURITY FEATURES

Because authority control activities can have broad ramifications in a large database with an online public access catalog (OPAC), security is very important. NOTIS security functions are both record and command specific. When a staff member signs on to the NOTIS system, the system identifies which technical services unit they are in, and which types of records they can create and/or update. For example, a staff member may be authorized to create and edit bibliographic records but have no access to authority records except to search and display. Furthermore, within a bibliographic or authority record, a staff member may have access to certain groups of fields but not to others.

The security module also controls which staff members can issue the commands which result in global heading changes or the designation of a master authority record.

FUTURE DEVELOPMENTS

NOTIS is in the process of testing a completely new design for authority control, the Merged Heading Index Project. The design and programming for this project is being carried out by Northwestern University Library Information Systems Development Office. The new module is now in production at Northwestern.

The significant design accomplishment of this project is the Merged Heading Index itself. This one index contains index entries for access points from both bibliographic records and authority records, arranged in "dictionary" order, e.g., names, subjects, and titles interfiled. The Merged Heading Index displays cross-references from the authority records to staff and patrons searching the index. Index entries are added to and removed from the index online in real time.

The searching capabilities of this index are also a significant enhancement. Now a staff member can view the entire index, as a dictionary file, or request specific subsets, such as author, title, subject, or series. The display of information from the Heading Use Codes of the authority record also facilitates staff use of the new index.

The Merged Heading Index will also be used to provide conflict detection reports to staff for authority control purposes. These reports will indicate discrepancies between bibliographic and authority records.

The excellent design of the Merged Heading Index lays the base for many future developments, such as search qualification, catalog-based searching, and enhanced global heading changes.

Name Authority in a NOTIS Environment — Auburn University Libraries

Helen Goldman
David M. Smith

SUMMARY. During the years 1984-85, the arrival of an integrated automated library system (NOTIS) forced Auburn University Libraries to reevaluate the status of its name authority system. Central to the evaluation process was the preservation of the major investment made in the card name authority file as a result of AACR2. To achieve this, a process of migrating the valuable information from the card file into an online environment was developed. The final result of this process was a new authority structure with current and potential capabilities superior to the previous manual system.

INTRODUCTION

The modern name authority era began at Auburn University Libraries with the advent of the second edition of the *Anglo-American Cataloguing Rules* (AACR2) in January of 1981. At this time the Cataloging Department (Monographic) made the decision to abandon the existing card name authority file (OLDNAF) and to establish a new card name authority file (AACR2 NAF) with only AACR2 forms of name. The OLDNAF was incomplete and had been created over a period of several decades without a great deal of consistency or direction. The public card catalog was, in fact, regarded as the authority for name headings during this period and

Helen Goldman, MLS (1984) University of South Carolina, is Catalog Maintenance Librarian, and David M. Smith, MLS (1967) Emory University, is Head of the Cataloging Department, Ralph Brown Draughon Library, Auburn University Libraries, Auburn, AL 36849-5606.

was normally checked in lieu of OLDNAF. AACR2 NAF grew rapidly from 1981 through 1984 and eventually reached a total of 100,000 cards. Part of this rapid growth was due to a Cataloging Department policy to establish a name authority record in AACR2 NAF for every new name heading, a practice later abandoned as impractical and unnecessary.

Auburn purchased Northwestern University's NOTIS automated library system in late 1983 and began to plan for the implementation of the technical services module. Part of the process included a review of the AACR2 NAF system begun almost three years earlier. The spring and summer of 1984 were spent in this review and also in the loading of 240,000 bibliographic records from Auburn's 1975-83 OCLC archival tapes. These records formed the initial online bibliographic file (NOTISFILE). During this period the decision was made to close the card catalog and to cease ordering catalog cards from OCLC at the end of November 1984. In order to access all library materials added after that date, the public would use the NOTIS public online catalog (LUIS). Bibliographic records for these new materials would be downloaded[1] individually via NOTIS software from OCLC directly into NOTISFILE.

EVALUATION OF THE NAME AUTHORITY PROCESS
(January-October 1984)

The major questions considered in the evaluation of the name authority process are described below.

1. *What is the feasibility of obtaining a vendor authority upgrade of NOTISFILE and the resulting name authority tapes?* Auburn determined that an authority upgrade of NOTISFILE was impractical until the late 1980s due to a major vendor retrospective conversion project that was scheduled to begin in the fall of 1984. The vendor was expected to convert over 275,000 records during the period from 1984 through 1988. A delay in any system-wide authority upgrade seemed appropriate until the completion of this project and the stabilization of the quality of input into the database. Secondly, there was concern about the compatibility of vendor-produced name authority tapes with the NOTIS authority software. Auburn was

aware of one NOTIS institution which had difficulty in fully integrating name authority tapes into their local system. Finally, most of the available funds for automation activities were being expended for the initial charges to acquire the NOTIS software and related hardware and to employ a library Automation Manager.

2. *What are the current and potential capabilities of the NOTIS authority software?* The capability of successfully loading online name authority records did not exist at Auburn in 1984. This was due to a lack of experience with the NOTIS system and to the higher priority given to the implementation of the acquisitions and cataloging modules of the system. However, information gathered from the early NOTIS documentation, from the 1984 NOTIS Users' Group Meeting, and from communication with Northwestern University Library's Head of Catalog Management, William Garrison, convinced Auburn that the NOTIS authority system had excellent potential.

Many desirable features of the online authority system were identified during this time. Among them were the ability to access the authority file from any *staff* NOTIS terminal, to make global heading changes, to make cross references index specific, and to download Library of Congress authority records from OCLC into NOTIS. Future NOTIS programming was scheduled to allow the name authority system to interact with LUIS via the "Merged Headings" software.

3. *What is the current availability of Cataloging Department personnel to operate the name authority system?* The staff assigned to name authority control had grown dramatically as a result of the impact of AACR2. The Authority Unit increased from one to three support staff between 1981 and 1984. As the result of a departmental reorganization, the Unit became part of the newly created Catalog Maintenance Section and reported to the Catalog Maintenance Librarian rather than to the Head of the Cataloging Department. The availability of a middle management position to direct and support the Unit's goals proved invaluable in the establishment of an online authority system. Consequently, options which required a considerable investment in staff were then feasible.

DECISIONS FROM THE NAME
AUTHORITY EVALUATION PROCESS
(November 1984)

Three decisions were reached as a result of the evaluation of the name authority process: a local online name authority file would be created; it would be supplemented by comparing new name headings to the NOTISFILE; and priority would be given to upgrading records in the NOTISFILE.

More specifically, it was decided the Authority Unit would begin, as soon as possible, the creation of an operational local NOTIS online name authority file (NOTIS NAF). The decision to create this file was reached after careful consideration of the issues reviewed above, including the rationale used by Northwestern University Library in deciding to load their own authority file.[2] The NOTIS NAF would be created both by adding records for appropriate name headings for new materials and also by systematically adding the retrospective name headings from the AACR2 NAF. Some names would be keyed into the NOTIS NAF manually, but most of the current and retrospective records were available in the Library of Congress name authority file on OCLC and could be downloaded into the NOTIS NAF. The headings in the NOTISFILE would be used as a supplement to the AACR2 NAF and the NOTIS NAF. This would permit the Authority Unit to accept as authoritative any new name heading that was present in a consistent form in NOTISFILE. This concept roughly paralleled the pre-AACR2 policy of bypassing the OLDNAF and instead using the public card catalog as the authority source. An ongoing enhancement of NOTISFILE would result from this checking process as conflicts were discovered and corrected. This process would also reduce pressure on the Unit to develop the NOTIS NAF overnight. Adoption of this premise would guarantee an improving level of consistency in NOTISFILE by introducing no *new* name headings without review by the Unit or a cataloger.

Thus, the decision was made to direct the major focus of the Authority Unit toward upgrading the quality of NOTISFILE as quickly as possible. This upgrading of the NOTISFILE would be done somewhat at the expense of the authority structure in the public card catalog, which was becoming increasingly obsolete as time progressed. This decision recognized that staff resources were finite and that improving NOTISFILE would only be delayed by continuing maintenance of the public card catalog. Once the corresponding record had been correctly entered in NOTISFILE the Cataloging staff would be allowed to pull and discard catalog cards with obsolete or incorrect name headings. This practice would not only avoid the costly and time-consuming process of pulling, correcting and refiling cards, but would also encourage increased public use of LUIS.

INTERIM AUTHORITY CONTROL
(December 1984-September 1985)

In the fall of 1984, following the decision to utilize the NOTIS authority online software, the Authority Unit closed the AACR2 NAF. This action paralleled the closing of the public card catalog. As a reaction to this change, the Unit began to recognize both the freedoms and problems which online systems can provide. Since it was no longer required to manually correct public catalog cards as a result of authority problems, the Unit focused completely on improving the consistency of the indexes in NOTISFILE.

The Unit's initial attempt to create a *test* name authority file in NOTIS was not successful. Because of inexperience and a misunderstanding of the NOTIS documentation, approximately one hundred authority records were inadvertently downloaded directly into NOTISFILE. It soon became apparent that the records should have been placed in a separate subsystem defined exclusively for authority records. This setback and a vacancy in the Catalog Maintenance Librarian position forced the suspension of this effort for several months. However, the Unit continued to modify the manual authority control processes in preparation for the ultimate goal of an online name authority system.

As mentioned above, the closing of AACR2 NAF was fundamental to this preparation process. Instead of typing new AACR2 NAF cards, a temporary file of Library of Congress name authority printouts and local name authority workforms was begun to document this activity until the arrival of the NOTIS NAF. This file had an expected life span of only a few months, but its purpose was to maintain a transitional record of name authority activity which could be carried forward into the NOTIS NAF. The typing of *all* cross references also ended with the closing of AACR2 NAF, and the temporary printout file was the *single* repository of local name authority information from December 1984 until the creation of the NOTIS NAF in the fall of 1985. In addition, the Unit compared each new printout against AACR2 NAF to insure that it would not become obsolete during the interim period.

In June 1985 the new Catalog Maintenance Librarian recommended the creation of a second test file. Approval was granted based on the resolution of the problems that had caused the first test file to fail in 1984 and coordination between the Authority Unit, Auburn University Libraries' Automation Manager, and NOTIS personnel. Five hundred test authority records representing as much diversity as possible were loaded during the summer. This experimentation worked well and many questions were answered concerning the feasibility of downloading authority records from OCLC and the inputting of local authority records.

CREATION OF THE NOTIS NAF
(October-December 1985)

The major remaining step in creating the third and final test file was to set aside the requisite online storage space for the NOTIS authority subsystem. The lack of available space had been a partial cause of the problems with Auburn's first test file in 1984. Auburn University Libraries' Automation Manager was able to provide adequate file space in the fall of 1985. If the loading process went as expected, it was the intent of the Automation Manager and the Authority Unit to convert this third test file into the NOTIS NAF.

The downloading of name authority records from the AACR2 NAF into the third test file began in October 1985 and followed a strict alphabetical arrangement. That is, only after all AACR2 NAF entries for a particular letter had been downloaded were the authority records from the temporary printout file for the same letter added. Also during this period, the use of limited time on the downloading terminals was maximized by conducting offline comparisons between headings in the AACR2 NAF and the temporary authority printout file. The downloading process thus progressed smoothly during October and November, and the transition was made from the test to the live NOTIS NAF on December 2, 1985.

Pleased by the NOTIS NAF's development, the Authority Unit began to promote this system. Discussions were held with the catalogers to gauge their expectations for the NOTIS NAF and specifically to determine how the system could utilize their submitted authority workforms. An orientation workshop for all catalogers in the Cataloging and Serials Departments was held in January 1986. Following this workshop the Unit composed and distributed documentation outlining name authority duties and responsibilities of the Unit and the catalogers.

The NOTIS NAF was also introduced to the public service librarians via the Auburn University Libraries' automation publication *NOTIS NOTES, etc.* Unfortunately, due to security restrictions, files which existed in the technical services mode could not display on the LUIS-only terminals in public services areas. However, each public service department had a restricted terminal that could access the NOTIS NAF. Feedback from public service staff members indicated that they were interested in the NOTIS NAF as a means of providing a syndetic structure to LUIS.

CURRENT NOTIS NAME AUTHORITY PRACTICE
(1986 to the present)

Auburn's current name authority procedure is very similar to the one installed in October of 1985. New materials still arrive in the Authority Unit accompanied by printouts of the bibliographic record as downloaded by the Acquisitions Department. However, the initial authority checkpoint is now the NOTIS NAF instead of the NOTISFILE. This change was made in the spring of 1986 in recognition of the growing size and utility of the NOTIS NAF, and also to revise it on a daily basis with up-to-date forms of name from the Library of Congress bibliographic printouts. If changes in forms of name are discovered, the existing NOTIS NAF record is replaced by downloading the revised Library of Congress name authority record. The hit rate of name headings for new materials in the NOTIS NAF has increased from 6.8% in July 1986 to 29.3% in February 1988. Name headings not located in NOTIS NAF continue to be checked against the NOTISFILE.

If a name heading on the bibliographic printout is a match in either the NOTIS NAF or NOTISFILE, it is coded on the printout by the source of verification[3] and delivered to the appropriate cataloger. All non-hits and conflicts from the NOTIS-based review are routed to the staff member checking against the national utility, the OCLC Library of Congress Name Authority File (OCLC/LC/NAF). Name headings verified in the OCLC/LC/NAF with AACR2 forms of name are coded on the bibliographic printout by the cataloging rules used to establish the heading.[4] The presence of cross references on the authority record dictates the next course of action. OCLC/LC/NAF records without cross references are not downloaded into NOTIS NAF because this offers no improvement over the verification obtained from the indexes of NOTISFILE. Conversely, OCLC/LC/NAF records with cross references are printed out and sorted for later downloading into NOTIS NAF. Direct transfer of OCLC/LC/NAF records into NOTIS NAF is not attempted during the routine verification workflow.

Once *all* name headings have been established the materials are then delivered to the appropriate catalogers. Records with name headings in conflict with NOTISFILE are routed to the Authority Unit Library Assistant with any supporting OCLC/LC/NAF printouts. These conflicts are resolved by the Library Assistant and, if necessary, the Catalog Maintenance Librarian. All headings that are not located in one of the authority sources (the NOTIS NAF, NOTISFILE, OCLC/LC/NAF), or have unresolved conflicts are routed to the catalogers with an annotated name authority workform for a final decision.

Another major consideration of the Authority Unit is the placement of name headings within the indexes of NOTIS. NOTIS authority records have more fixed field elements than those of the Library of Congress. These additional elements address the use of the heading in the subject, author, and series indexes. Authority Unit staff check all indexes for each heading before downloading into the NOTIS NAF. Also the specific indexes utilized are recorded on the name authority workforms.

The procedures described above have proven to be efficient. The Authority Unit reviewed the name headings for approximately 35,000 titles in 1985/86, and 52,000 in 1986/87. The increase for 1986/87 was due to growth in the materials budget and also the absorption of the "monographs in series" materials from the Serials Department in the fall of 1986. The Unit's improved productivity allowed it to handle this 48% increase in incoming materials without significant delays and to continue the downloading of the name headings from AACR2 NAF.

GOALS

While the NOTIS NAF has been quite successful, there are a number of goals that have yet to be achieved. Chief among these is the NOTIS "Merged Headings" program referred to above. A future provision of this software by NOTIS will close the most serious gap in the authority system—the interface with LUIS. It will, for the first time, allow the library user to reap the full benefits of the capabilities of the NOTIS system.

A second goal will be full implementation of the NOTIS global change program. Auburn, because of local programming constraints, does not yet have access to the global change features of NOTIS. Fortunately, the needed changes in erroneous name headings have been made successfully by other, though less efficient, methods. In a similar vein, Auburn plans to make even greater use of the batch programs presently available via the NOTIS software, including the new and dropped name and subject headings lists.

Finally, the Authority Unit soon expects to be able to incorporate the Library of Congress subject headings into its system. This incorporation will occur once our retrospective downloading of the AACR2 NAF is completed and will allow us to devote the same level of standardization for subjects as that being achieved by the name authority system.

CONCLUSION

The Authority Unit has nearly completed the transfer of the name authority records from the AACR2 NAF into the NOTIS NAF that began in October 1985. The headings for the letters A-V have been reviewed and individually downloaded into the NOTIS NAF. In addition, the loading of name authority records generated by the review of name headings for currently received material is up-to-date. The NOTIS NAF currently contains 51,000 records to support the NOTISFILE's 725,000 bibliographic records.

The checking of each name heading for new materials by the Authority Unit has proven to be an extremely valuable standardization function for the NOTISFILE. As a result of conflicts identified in this checking process, an average of 928 bibliographic records were corrected by the Unit staff each month in 1985/86. The monthly average increased to 1126 for 1986/87 and to 1539 by March 1988.

In sum, the impact of the NOTIS NAF over the past two and one-half years has been very significant. Staff members now have convenient online access to a substantial local authority file within the NOTIS system. The availability and localization of the NOTIS NAF offers a major improvement over the OCLC/LC/NAF. The near-term value of the file has been its ability to free the catalogers from routine name authority matters and to allow them to concentrate on the difficult decisions regarding the form of name. The long-term value has been the creation of a collection-specific online name authority file that lays a solid framework for the myriad of applications in the future. There is a strong sense at Auburn University Libraries that the decision to build the NOTIS NAF based on local authority data was the correct one.

NOTES

1. "Downloading" refers to the NOTIS OCLC/Telex Transfer Program. This process transfers machine readable data from OCLC into NOTIS by using a Telex model 476L display terminal to receive the data from an OCLC terminal line-by-line in the same manner as a printer. The Telex terminal is, in fact, cabled to the OCLC serial printer port (port 2 on the OCLC M300).

2. Northwestern elected to create their online authority file locally after determining that using the Library of Congress Name Headings tapes would not meet

their needs. The LCNAF tapes matched Northwestern's manual name authority file only 10% of the time and would have required local adaptation of cross references too expensive to entertain. (Elisabeth Janakiev and William Garrison, "Retrospective Conversion of Authority Records." In *Retrospective Conversion: From Cards to Computer.* Edited by Anne G. Adler and Elizabeth A. Baber, pp. 303-310. Ann Arbor, MI: Pierian Press, 1984.)

3. Codes of verification on NOTIS include: NT = present and consistent in NOTISFILE; NTC = present but inconsistent in NOTISFILE; NAF = present in NOTIS NAF.

4. Code of verification on OCLC/LC/NAF include: C = present in OCLC/LC/NAF as AACR2; D = present in OCLC/LC/NAF as AACR2 compatible; A = present in OCLC/LC/NAF established under rules earlier than AACR1; B = present in OCLC/LC/NAF established under AACR1; 0 = no confirmation in NOTISFILE, NOTIS NAF, OCLC/LC/NAF. To suggest reappraisal of name headings coded with A or B, OCLC/LC/NAF printouts and an Auburn authority workform are sent to the cataloger. Name headings coded 0 are accompanied by an Auburn authority workform.

Authority Control
on the Geac
Bibliographic Processing System

Michel Ridgeway

SUMMARY. This article describes the implementation of authority control on the Geac Bibliographic Processing System. An appendix includes screen displays and search results for headings under authority control in an online public access catalog.

Authority control as implemented on the Geac Bibliographic Processing System is designed to accomplish the following:

1. Provide the online catalog user with the syndetic structure of the authority record in a simple and straightforward manner.
2. Establish control over appropriate headings as they exist or are added to a local system.

Geac's Bibliographic Processing System represents a rewriting of the catalog management software based on authority control as an integral part of the system design, rather than superimposed over existing software.

The following article describes the use of the system. It also addresses concerns about implementing automated authority control in a local system.

Michel Ridgeway is responsible for Product Marketing at Geac Computers, Inc., 515 North Washington St., Alexandria, VA 22314. The views expressed in this article are his, and not those of Geac Computers, Inc., or its affiliates. Mr. Ridgeway is a graduate of Bowdoin College and received an MSLS from Columbia University.

THE ONLINE CATALOG

The following are the goals for Geac's online catalog with authority control.

1. The user does not need to understand authority control as a concept but is led through the catalog by the manifestations of the internal authority structure.
2. If the user matches or views the variant heading (SEE reference), the user does not have to key the established heading.
3. Related headings (SEE ALSO references) may or may not be needed by the user, therefore the selection of related headings is at the user's discretion.
4. Blind headings are supported on the system to serve as useful information in the cataloging process but blind headings are masked from the public catalog display.
5. The display of notes from the authority record is available to the online catalog user.
6. The transition from an online catalog without authority control to an online catalog with authority control is without major differences to the user.

Online Catalog References

A significant departure from the traditional "SEE" reference of a card file format came with the introduction of what Geac calls the "Known as:" reference (see Screens 1-4 in Appendix). In this implementation, a user entering a search string which matches a variant form (i.e., 4XX authority tag) in the appropriate index is shown the search string the user entered, the variant form matched, and that this variant form of the heading is "Known as" the established form.

The result of a user's search on the Geac Online Public Access Catalog (OPAC) may be at three levels: the index level (no match against existing headings, closest matches shown), the citation level (two or more bibliographic citations exist and match the search string), and the record level (the search string matches a heading which exists on a single record in the database). "Known as:" references are shown at all levels. Some sample screens (1-4) are shown in the Appendix, but as a brief example, if a user enters "Clemens, Samuel," the system responds that "Clemens, Samuel Langhorne, 1835-1910" matches the search and that the author is "Known as: Twain, Mark," and the bibliographic citations are listed. The user is not required to make a further search but need only select the heading or examine the citations.

Related headings (SEE ALSO references) are handled differently. Every search result provides the user with a context-specific set of prompted commands which may be used (see Screens 5-8 in Appendix). When a user matches or selects a heading which also has related headings, the display adds an additional prompt "REF — see related references" (see Screen 5 in Appendix). When a user enters "REF," the screen displays an alphabetic list of headings with the number of bibliographic citations held by the library for each heading (see Screen 6 in Appendix).

Again, the user need only select from the list, not reenter any further searches. It should also be pointed out that the use of the "REF" command may also be performed on headings located through earlier use of the "REF" command (see Screens 7 and 8 in Appendix). Therefore, the user may explore the full syndetic structure of the authority database and locate desired materials without an elaborate command syntax.

Related references often occur only at the higher or highest level of the heading. This means the user will not see lower level headings at the "SEE ALSO" screen. However, if the user selects a related heading and then commands the "IND" or Index Display, then the heading selected is shown with the lower level headings alphabetically listed (see Screen 9 in Appendix). The user has been shifted in the index from the original search key through the selection of the related heading. Geac's resolution of the reference structure of SEE and SEE ALSO headings was therefore straightforwardly addressed.

Online Catalog Authority Notes

The display of authority record notes in the online catalog was not as easily resolved. The entry of notes into the authority record are of particular value to the scholarly researcher or a cataloger but not necessarily of use to the broad spectrum of online catalog users that Geac serves. It was therefore decided to make the authority note display command, "NOT," a "hidden" command, that is, not prompted as an available command to the user. This is in keeping with some other online catalog commands, such as the "MAR" or MARC display command which causes the online catalog to display the record in MARC format, useful for internal users, but not obvious for the public.

The basic problem that authority notes present is that the wording of most notes is not written for the general public. Greater care must be taken in the creation and editing of the authority notes if they are intended for public use. Jargon should be avoided. History and scope notes occur on a small percentage of records. The use of notes is a possible area where further study should be undertaken before they are a part of online catalogs.

AUTOMATED AUTHORITY PROCESSING

The public interface to the online catalog is the result of considerable processing on the system to create record linkages which allow navigation by the user from one heading to another. Examples of automated authority processing include the loading and indexing of MARC authority records on a local system, the matching and linking of bibliographic headings to authority headings, and the review and analysis of the various reports created.

Many libraries have recently engaged in retrospective conversion of their catalog data to MARC format. However, the impetus toward record conversion and the creation of MARC-based bibliographic files was not always accompanied by simultaneous authority record creation, since the capability of matching against a machine-readable authority file has been recent. Consequently, for many libraries, this matching must be done retrospectively against an authority file and the matched authority records supplied for loading into the local system. Following the MARC authority record load and the attendant problems of reconciliation, the library must determine a means of matching and loading authorities on an ongoing basis.

Geac's authority processing software must accommodate this reality. The following conditions apply to many Geac libraries:

1. large bibliographic files (250,000 to over 1 million records, with most in the 400,000 to 700,000 range),
2. online catalogs in a live environment, with the requirement of availability even beyond the library's hours of operation,
3. large numbers of authority records created by vendor matching and in order to synchronize the matching, the local system replicates the vendor match algorithms,
4. varying requirements among libraries; e.g., one library's perceived greatest need is in subject authority control, another's is corporate names,
5. the likelihood of a high percentage of unmatched headings (over 50%),
6. the ongoing requirement to add new materials to the system at current or increased rates,
7. the desirability of accomplishing as much as possible through machine processing, rather than costly staff intervention.

This is a daunting list. To overcome the concerns associated with these conditions requires careful planning and special recognition of the ambitious nature of the project. It requires a strong commitment on the library's part and a willingness to address the particular problems of online authority processing.

To facilitate online authority processing Geac provides several approaches for libraries.

1. The mechanism used to bring a local system into correspondence with a vendor's match algorithm is a system table that may be edited locally. The table reflects the library's determination of which fields and which data within those fields are subject to authority control. Validation of tags, indicators, and subfield codes is also managed through a locally defined table.
2. To prevent disruption of online catalog service, Geac can run automated authority processing while the online catalog is available.
3. Local authority records may be created from existing biblio-

graphic data. Geac allows control over existing unmatched headings and permits local editing to upgrade those records.

4. Automated authority processing generates numerous reports to document the machine's activities and to alert the system users to work that requires human attention. For example, lucid and organized system generated reports provide data on unmatched and conflicting headings that require human reconciliation.

5. The implementation is designed to accomplish as much processing as possible before authorities are "live," that is to say, in use and manipulated by the online cataloging module, as well as available in the public online catalog.

In an ideal automated authority processing situation, the MARC authority and bibliographic records would be loaded on the local system contemporaneously. Authorization matches would then be done, the reports analyzed, flips made, and the online catalog would be live with its headings fully linked and authorized. This is a lengthy process. It requires a long lead time generally not politically possible in the current library environment, which expects a quick and visible return on the considerable investment made to purchase a local system.

Given this political reality a live online catalog without automated authority control, and implementing authority control subsequently, will draw out the process. However, service to the public will be available but without the complete assistance of the authority syndetic structure.

There are two types of processing available to Geac users: batch processing and online operations. In general, batch processing is performed by the system, and online operations are performed by an operator at a terminal.

Batch Processing

Batch processing refers to having a program handle a number of records sequentially with the program doing all the processing without operator intervention after the batch is initiated. Many library operations lend themselves to batch operations since the record array is sequential and the program processing is the same for each record. Examples of batch processing for authorities are the loading of authority records from a MARC tape and the reporting of the match process. Procedures done in batch are usually performed at the system level. Geac, in recognition of the reality that batch processing may be lengthy, has made concentrated efforts to permit system level batch processing in real time, that is the changes to the database may be done in batch while the online catalog and cataloging are available. Through priority job assignment on the system, the batch may run at a lower priority to insure that response time does not degenerate for online catalog users.

The results of authority batch processing are as follows:

1. Authority records are loaded. If a library purchases a matched, de-duplicated set of authorities from a vendor, no error condition checking need be done at this point and the load may be done more quickly. The only records to be reported at this stage would be records which were supplied in a corrupt state.

   Another time-saving step which may be taken by the library and the authority record supplier is to provide the bibliographic record number, tag number, and tag occurrence number that matched with the authority record supplied. From this information Geac can build the authority-bibliographic links directly insuring that the local linkages will be the same as the vendor's match algorithm.

   For authority records which require de-duping and checking against existing headings, Geac will report illogical conditions and also provide duplicate authority record checking by record number. The following inconsistencies are reported:

Submitted record		*Existing database*
Authorized form	matches	Authorized form
Authorized form	matches	Variant form
Related heading	matches	Variant form
Variant form	matches	Authorized form
Variant form	matches	Related heading

2. Reports are produced. The bibliographic headings may be tested against the authority headings all at once or by record

number ranges. The software tests and reports both unmatched headings and headings which match a variant form (flip). The system can make the flip if desired.

3. Provisional authority records are created. Again, this may be done on the whole database or by individual record ranges. It is recommended that this be done on record ranges, since the system will create authorities from the unmatched headings. A review of these will undoubtedly reveal many headings in error, generally through typographical errors or incomplete data. These bibliographic record headings will make equally erroneous authority records and should be corrected before provisional authorities are created.

Online Operations

The online operations are those authority procedures which are accomplished by a cataloging operator at a terminal accessing the database. Aspects of authority processing which are relevant to online applications are:

1. Security. Bibliographic and authority records may be added, changed, or deleted only by a cataloger with appropriate permissions and assigned cataloging level.
2. Searching. Location of appropriate headings may be facilitated by restricting searches to authority headings only or further limiting the search to personal name or corporate name authorities.
3. Editing capabilities. Memorizing records for subsequent display, capturing a tag from one record and inserting it in another, resequencing tags, and renumbering tags are all special editing features added to ease record manipulation.
4. Making the bibliographic-authority link. A request to link a heading consists of the link command, a system table lookup to determine the link-type (for example, headings in bibliographic X00 tags link to authority 100 tags), a search of the authority indexes, the presentation of the link candidate(s), the confirmation of the link, and the changing of the bibliographic data to the authority data.
5. Provisional authority creation. The system can generate a new

authority record by a command, creating an authority record from the existing data of a bibliographic tag.

6. Global update. Changing the authorized form of a heading automatically updates the heading in linked fields within the bibliographic record.

7. Local data entry. Authority records may be added through keying the authority data into the database on a locally-defined authority format workform.

Ongoing Authority Processing

The loading of new authorities requires another type of authorities processing. In this case, a type of "reverse" authorization occurs, where added authorities are matched not only against the existing authorities but also against the existing bibliographic headings.

It is expected that sources of authority data will continue to expand as more and more libraries require authority records for their local systems. Currently, tape suppliers are the most common, but advances in technology such as CD-ROM and the Linked Systems Project offer likely sources for authority data in the future.

Problems in Authorities Processing

The problems of authority processing are those which cannot be reconciled by program processing and require human intervention. These occur because of inconsistencies between the bibliographic and authority records with regard to format structure, AACR2 mandated changes, and the data supplied by the Library of Congress on its authority records.

The number of authority headings involved in a project requiring that all headings be under authority control is staggering. In fact, it is likely that libraries would require more authority records than bibliographic records if all unique headings were given their own authority record. If such a structure is desired, it may be beneficial to phase in the implementation of authority control, such as beginning with control of only name headings or subjects to reduce the size of reports and focus on a manageable subset of the catalog headings.

The inconsistencies between the MARC Bibliographic formats and the MARC Authority format also create a regular problem in flipping, especially with regard to tag indicators. For example, the 730 tag in the bibliographic format uses the first indicator for non-filing characters and the second indicator for type of added entry. The first indicator may be derived from the second indicator of the 130 tag of the authority record but the type of added entry is not on the authority record and may not be derived.

The problem of matching 100/240 bibliographic tag combinations to a single authority 100 tag has led Geac to create an elaborate syntax structure to allow matching of this type of bibliographic data with authority data. The 100/240 structure is an anachronism from the printed card environment.

Many series heading changes were mandated by AACR2. Headings which were formerly personal or corporate names became title entries. In general, flipping data within a field does not necessarily mean that the tag changes, but managing this type of series change requires that the tag also changes. The situation does not readily lend itself to resolution by system processing since it may be desired to retain the data from the original submitted field on the record as a 490 tag rather than just flipping it and assigning a new tag.

Conference headings for individual conferences in a series often are not supplied by the Library of Congress on its authority records. However, the main part of the heading may still be examined for consistency. The variable parts of the heading, namely date, place and year may be excluded from authority control. On the Geac system the library may choose between matching the entire heading or only part of the heading.

CONCLUSION

In summary, Geac's approach to authority control has been to address the needs of the user of the online catalog and the complex problems of database loads and ongoing heading and record maintenance. The process is still new and continued progress and enhancements are to be expected. The experience has been illustrative of the specialized nature of library automation procedures. It has required a careful definition of requirements, a thorough identification of exceptions, and the generous cooperation and advice of many Geac customers, here gratefully acknowledged.

APPENDIX

Screen 1. Author search for "SMITH"; no exact match; index display with "Known as: " references.

```
_____
|                                                               |
| 701 THE UNIVERSITY LIBRARY   - GEAC LIBRARY SYSTEM - ALL *AUTHOR SEARCH |
|                                                               |
| Your Author: SMITH                      Matches at least  25  authors |
|                                                               |
|                                                   No. of citations |
|                                                   in entire catalog |
|                                                               |
| 1 Smith, A. G. Cairns-                                        |
|   Known as: Cairns-Smith, A. G.                               |
| 2 Smith, A. G. R.                                          1  |
|   Known as:  Smith, Alan Gordon,Rae.                          |
| 3 Smith, A. Merriman, 1913-                               1  |
| 4 Smith, A. Merriman, 1913-1970.                          2  |
| 5 Smith, Adolphe,                                         1  |
| 6 Smith, Al, 1873-1944                                    1  |
|   Known as:  Smith, Alfred Emanuel, 1873-1944.                |
| 7 Smith, Alan, 1925-                                      1  |
| 8 Smith, Alan, 1925 (Oct. 31)-                            1  |
|                                                           3  |
|                                                               |
| Type a number to see more information -OR-                    |
| FOR - move forward in this list    BAC - move backward in this list |
| CAT - begin a new search           CMD - see additional commands |
|                                                               |
| Enter number or code: 1                       Then press SEND |
|_____|
```

Screen 2. Author search; exact match; single citation record display. Match is against variant form.

```
[                                                                              ]
[  001 THE UNIVERSITY LIBRARY   - GEAC LIBRARY SYSTEM -  ALL *AUTHOR SEARCH     ]
[                                                               Matches    1 citation  ]
[  Your Author: SMITH A G CAIRNS                                               ]
[      matches: Smith, A. G. Cairns-                                           ]
[    known as: Cairns-Smith, A. G.                                             ]
[                                                                              ]
[  AUTHOR:  Cairns-Smith, A. G.                                                ]
[  TITLE:   The life puzzle: on crystals and organisms and on the possibility of >  ]
[  IMPRINT: [Toronto] University of Toronto Press [1971]                       ]
[                                                                              ]
[                          Loan   Call             Cpy                         ]
[            Location      Type   Number            #   Status                 ]
[                                                                              ]
[            UNILIB/ART    2WEEK  QH325.C13 1971    1   In Library.            ]
[            PUBLIB/MAIN   2WEEK  QH325.C13 1971    2   In Library             ]
[            PUBLIB/WEST   CHIFIC QH325.C13 1971    3   In Library             ]
[                                                                              ]
[            FUL - see complete citation      IND - see list of headings       ]
[            CAT - begin a new search         CMD - see additional commands     ]
[                                                                              ]
[            Enter code CAT                            Then press SEND          ]
[                                                                              ]
```

Screen 3. Author search; exact match against variant form; citation display.

```
001 THE UNIVERSITY LIBRARY    - GEAC LIBRARY SYSTEM -  ALL *AUTHOR SEARCH

Your Author: A.L.A.                                    matches     9 citations
   matches: A.L.A.
   known as: American library Association.

Ref# Author                      Title                                        Date
  1 American library associati>  A.L.A. portrait index;                       1906
  2 American library associati>  A.L.A. rules for filing catalog car>         1942
  3 American Library Associati>  The acquisition of library material>         1973
  4 American Library Associati>  American libraries.                          1970
  5 American Library Associati>  Anglo-American cataloging rules.             1970
  6 American Library Associati>  Anglo-American cataloging rules.             1974
  7 American Library Associati>  Guide to reference books                     1967
  8 American Library Associati>  The library and information network>         1963
  9 American Library Associati>  Proceedings.                                 1971


Type a number to see associated information -OR-
   IND - see list of headings             CAT - begin a new search
   CMD - see additional commands

Enter number or code: CAT                               Then press SEND
```

Screen 4. Subject search; exact match; identical variant form on separate authority records.

```
┌───────────────────────────────────────────────────────────────────┐
│ 001 THE UNIVERSITY LIBRARY    - GEAC LIBRARY SYSTEM -  ALL *SUBJECT SEARCH
│
│ Your Subject: ANCESTRY                                Matches   2  subjects
│
│                                                         No. of citations
│                                                         in entire catalog
│
│   1 Ancestry
│     Known as:  Genealogy                                      3
│   2 Ancestry
│     Known as:  Heredity                                      33
│
│
│
│ Type a number to see more information —OR—
│ FOR — move forward in this list        BAC — move backward in this list
│ CAT — begin a new search               CMD — see additional commands
│
│ Enter number or code: 2                               Then press SEND
└───────────────────────────────────────────────────────────────────┘
```

Screen 5. Citation display for "HEREDITY"; note that "REF" appears as a prompt.

```
001 THE UNIVERSITY LIBRARY  - GEAC LIBRARY SYSTEM -  ALL *SUBJECT SEARCH

                                              matches    33 citations

Ref# Author                       Title                                     Date
  1 Babcock, Ernest Brown, 187>   Genetics in relation to agriculture>      1927
  2 Bateson, William, 1861-192>   Mendel's principles of heredity,          1913
  3 Castle, William Ernest, 18>   Contributions to the genetics of th>      1932
  4 Clausen, Jens Christian, 1>   Experimental studies on the nature >      1940
  5 Clausen, Jens Christian, 1>   Experimental studies on the nature >      1940
  6 Crew, Francis Albert Eley,>   The genetics of sexuality in animal>      1927
  7 Darlington, Cyril Dean, 19>   Genetics and man                          1964
  8 Darwin, Charles Robert, 18>   The descent of man, and selection i>      1883
  9 Darwin, Charles Robert, 18>   The descent of man, and selection i>      1871
 10 Davenport, Charles Benedic>   Heredity in relation to eugenics,         1911
 11 Dunn, Leslie Clarence, 189>   Heredity and variation;                   1932
 12 Dunn, Leslie Clarence, 189>   Heredity, race, and society               1952

Type a number to see associated information —OR—
   IND — see list of headings        FOR — move forward in this list
-->REF — see related headings        CAT — begin a new search
   CMD — see additional commands
Enter number or code: REF                         Then press SEND
```

Screen 6. References for "HEREDITY"

```
┌─────────────────────────────────────────────────────────────────┐
│ 001 THE UNIVERSITY LIBRARY   - GEAC LIBRARY SYSTEM -  ALL *REFERENCES │
│                                                                   │
│ Your Subject: Heredity.                    has  14 reference(s)   │
│                                                                   │
│    See also:                               No. of citations       │
│                                            in entire catalog      │
│                                                                   │
│    1 Biometry                                      24             │
│    2 Chromosomes                                   11             │
│    3 Cytoplasmic inheritance                        4             │
│    4 Eugenics                                      20             │
│    5 Evolution                                    204             │
│    6 Genetics                                      48             │
│    7 Hybridization                                  3             │
│    8 Inheritance of acquired characters             2             │
│    9 Linkage (Genetics)                             2             │
│   10 Man — Constitution                             4             │
│   11 Mendel's law                                   2             │
│                                                                   │
│ Type a number to see more information —OR—                        │
│   IND — see list of headings        FOR — move forward in this list │
│   CAT — begin a new search          CMD — see additional commands │
│                                                                   │
│ Enter number or code: 5                          Then press SEND  │
└─────────────────────────────────────────────────────────────────┘
```

Screen 7. Citation display for "EVOLUTION"; selected from "HEREDITY" references.

```
001 THE UNIVERSITY LIBRARY    - GEAC LIBRARY SYSTEM -  ALL *SUBJECT SEARCH

                                                matches  204 citations


Ref# Author                         Title                                    Date
  1                                  Evolution in the light of modern kn>     1925
  2 Agassiz, Louis, 1807-1873.>      Methods of study in natural history>     1970
  3 Allen, Leslie Henri, 1887->      Bryan and Darrow at Dayton;              1925
  4 Asimov, Isaac, 1920-             The wellsprings of life.                 1960
  5 Association for the Study >      Evolutionary aspects of animal comm>     1962
  6 Avery, David F.                  Evolution of the iguanine lizards <>     1971
  7 Baitsell, George Alfred, 1>      The evolution of man;                    1922
  8 Barrell, Joseph, 1869-           The Evolution of the earth and its >     1918
  9 Bateson, William, 1861-192>      Mendel's principles of heredity,         1913
 10 Berg, Lev Semenovich, 1876>      Nomogenesis;                             1969
 11 Blair, W. Frank, 1912-           Evolution in the genus Bufo.             1972
 12 Blair, W. Frank, 1912-           Evolution in the genus Bufo.             1972


Type a number to see associated information -OR-
  IND - see list of headings           FOR - move forward in this list
  REF - see related headings           CAT - begin a new search
  CMD - see additional commands
Enter number or code: REF                            Then press SEND
```

Screen 8. References for "EVOLUTION"

```
|-------------------------------------------------------------------|
|                                                                   |
|  001 THE. UNIVERSITY LIBRARY   - GEAC LIBRARY SYSTEM -  ALL *REFERENCES  |
|                                                                   |
|  Your Subject: Evolution.                        has  29 reference(s)   |
|                                                                   |
|     See also:                                    No. of citations |
|                                                  in entire catalog|
|                                                                   |
|     1 Adaptation (Biology).                           30          |
|     2 Anatomy, Comparative                            16          |
|     3 Behavior evolution                               4          |
|     4 Biology                                         32          |
|     5 Color of animals                                10          |
|     6 Color of man                                     3          |
|     7 Embryology                                      21          |
|     8 Epigenesis                                       1          |
|     9 Ethics, Evolutionary                             1          |
|    10 Genetic psychology                               3          |
|    11 Genetics                                        48          |
|                                                                   |
|  Type a number to see more information -OR-                       |
|   IND - see list of headings      FOR - move forward in this list |
|   CAT - begin a new search        CMD - see additional commands   |
|                                                                   |
|  Enter number or code: IND                       Then press SEND  |
|                                                                   |
|-------------------------------------------------------------------|
```

Screen 9. Index display from "EVOLUTION" citations shows lower level headings.

```
001 THE UNIVERSITY LIBRARY   - GEAC LIBRARY SYSTEM -  ALL *SUBJECT SEARCH

                                                    No. of citations
                                                    in entire catalog

   1 Evolution.                                           204
   2 Evolution — Addresses, essays, lectures.              17
   3 Evolution and genetics.                                1
   4 Evolution — Bibliography.                              1
   5 Evolution, Chemical
     Known as: Chemical evolution                           3
   6 Evolution — Congresses.                               12
   7 Evolution — History.                                   5
   8 Evolution — History — Congresses.                      1
   9 Evolution — Juvenile literature.                       1
  10 Evolution — Marine.                                    1
  11 Evolution — Mathematics.                               2
  12 Evolution — Pictorial works.                           1

Type a number to see more information —OR—
FOR — move forward in this list     BAC — move backward in this list
CAT — begin a new search            CMD — see additional commands

Enter number or code: FOR           Then press SEND
```

Creating an Interactive Authority File for Names in the UCLA ORION System: Specifications and Decisions

George E. Gibbs
Diane Bisom

SUMMARY. The authors describe the creation of a linked authority system on the UCLA Library's ORION system. The computer specifications used to convert headings from the bibliographic file to authority records are given and the problems encountered in this process and the solutions decided upon are enumerated.

Linking the name headings from online bibliographic records with their authoritative forms stored in an online authority file is a much sought after capability of online catalogs. The UCLA Library online information system, ORION, provides such a linked file, called the Name Authority File. Derived from the headings on records in the bibliographic files, the file provides structured access to names and their associated cross references. Through a different set of commands, staff can access the authority records themselves and perform editing and global update functions. This article includes the specifications established to convert bibliographic headings into authority headings and the problems caused by the discrepancies between the MARC bibliographic and authority formats. It gives our solutions to these problems and sets forth the features of the linked file and the benefits derived from it.

George E. Gibbs is Head, Cataloging Division, University Research Library, University of California, Los Angeles. Diane Bisom is ORION User Services Librarian, University of California, Los Angeles.

BACKGROUND

In 1983 the cataloging units of the UCLA Library began entering name authority records in an online file in ORION.[1] This file consisted of records for personal, corporate, conference, and uniform title (including series) headings used as a main entry, added entry, or subject entry on bibliographic records being added to the database. Authority records for topical and geographic subjects were placed in a separate file. Most of the name authority records were copied from the Library of Congress Authority File mounted on the OCLC database; in the absence of LC authority records, locally created authority records were keyed. All records were keyed manually into the local authority file.

The online authority file was initially a stand-alone file with no links to the online bibliographic file, but with its creation, the relatively small, manual authority file for AACR2 headings was closed and all authority work for current cataloging moved online. While it was an improvement over the manual file because Boolean searching was possible, catalogers still had to conduct a separate search in order to access the information in the authority file. As a result, there was increased sentiment to link the bibliographic and authority files, not only for the ease of authority searching but also enhanced public access and for increased ease of maintenance which would be possible with a global change capability.

Several possible ways to create a link between the online name authority file and the bibliographic records were identified. The senior ORION system designer determined that the optimum method of establishing the linkage in ORION, given the basic structure of the system and the operating system of the IBM 3090 mainframe on which it operates, was to create a separate authority file made up of headings copied from records in the bibliographic file and to store the system number from the bibliographic records as part of the authority record.

SPECIFICATIONS

Specifications for the selection of the bibliographic fields and subfields which would be used to generate authority records for the linked name authority control module were developed by ORION User Services staff in consultation with the Library's Advisory Committee on Cataloging Policy (see Appendix I). Several online versions of this new file were created to test the specifications and to allow cataloging staff and others to review the generated records of filing arrangements, note problems, and recommend refinements. Through this process, a number of problematic situations involving indicators, series, and uniform titles, all discussed below, became apparent. The specifications for creating the file and the methods for updating it and the bibliographic records dynamically were refined via these test versions over a period of two years, until the module was completed in July 1986.

GENERAL DESCRIPTION

Appendix I gives the specifications which govern the transformation of headings from bibliographic records into authority records.

Headings for the authority file are selected from the three bibliographic files which are online in ORION—the monographic cataloging file (MC), the serials file (TC), and the monographic in-process (IP) file. As of January 1988 the monographic cataloging file consisted of 1,842,588 records; the serials file, 162,233 records; and the in-process file, 295,653 for a total of 2,300,474 bibliographic records. Headings from these records created 1,909,086 name authority records.

The program differentiates between works by (main and added entries) and works about (subject entries) and displays them separately under each authority heading. In Appendix I "x" is used to indicate works by and "y" is used to indicate works about.

The records from the monographic in-process (IP) file have several inherent problems: there are no subfield codes and in the early days of the file series were input as 400 rather than coded precisely and indicators were not recorded. Special default conditions have been defined for these in-process records.

All of the subfield codes listed in the SUBFIELD column in Appendix I are considered important enough to justify a separate entry in the Browse File. All of the other subfield codes, such as $e for relators, are ignored in file construction but retained in the bibliographic record in all cases, even after a global update. The listing of the subfield codes in the SUBFIELDS column is a listing of the order in which the subfield codes are generally found in bibliographic records. The delimiter symbol is represented by a "$" in ORION.

Thus, following the transformation specifications laid out in Appendix I

100 10 $a Cather, Willa, $d 1873-1947.
700 10 $a Cather, Willa, $d 1873-1947, $e comp.

from bibliographic records are both converted to

100 10 $a Cather, Willa, $d 1873-1947.

in the authority file. An untraced series from a bibliographic record, such as,

490 0 $a McGraw-Hill publications in city planning,

does not link in the name authority file, although the authority record is present and displays on staff terminals; while a traced series, such as,

440 0 $a AIP conference proceedings ; $v no. 68,

is converted to

130 00 $a AIP conference proceedings

in the authority file.

CREATING THE FILE

In order to create the file, headings were taken from the bibliographic records as indicated in the specifications in Appendix I. After the headings were normalized, identical headings were merged together. Each of the new authority records includes a locally defined field which contains the code for the ORION logical file in which the record resides, the sequential system number of the bibliographic record which has used the heading, and an "x" for works by the heading (1xx, 4xx, 7xx, and 8xx) and a "y" for works about the heading (6xx). The system number acts as the link for global update. A change in the authority file will automatically initiate a change in the bibliographic file and vice versa.

Following the pattern established in the manual catalog, the only headings which have full authority records are those for which we need to list cross references or those for which we need to record some piece of information, such as local usage information. The cross references listed in each of these authority records are "exploded" to create a separate entry in the authority file and are interfiled alphabetically among the headings. As part of the creation of the new linked name authority file, the headings in the first online Authority File were incorporated into the new online file. Figure 1 shows the result of an ORION browse name search.

Full authority records are entered into the file by one of two methods. Records from the Library of Congress Authority File mounted on the OCLC database are downloaded onto diskettes and then uploaded into ORION; original authority records created by UCLA Library staff are keyed directly into the online authority file. As each full authority record is entered into the file, an 035 field with the word "LOCK" is automatically added to the record. The presence of this word in the record prevents the automatic deletion of the authority record when there are no holdings posted against a heading, for example, when all titles are withdrawn. It also causes an asterisk to display next to the record with the full authority record on the results screen seen by UCLA Library staff. (See line R1 in Figure 1.) The asterisk identifies the authoritative form of heading in situations in which more than one version of the name appears in the file[2] and its presence is helpful in training paraprofessional staff to find the authoritative heading.

```
            EXAMPLE OF ORION BROWSE NAME RESULTS SCREEN
       CURRENT SEARCH: BNA WHARTON EDITH
   -HEADINGS CONTAINING ENTERED BROWSE TERM(S) - 12 RESULTS
            <-> NUMBER OF ONLINE ORION RECORDS CONTAINED IN EACH GROUP.
   R1 116  *Wharton, Edith, 1862-1937.
   R2   1   Wharton, Edith, 1862-1937. Ethan Frome.
   R3   1   Wharton, Edith, 1862-1937. Novels.  Selections.
   R4   1   Wharton, Edith, 1862-1937. Old maid.
   R5   3   Wharton, Edith, 1862-1937--Bibliography.
   R6   1   Wharton, Edith, 1862-1937--Biography.
   R7   9  +Wharton, Edith, 1862-1937--Criticism and interpretation.
        -   Wharton, Edith Newbold Jones, 1862-1937
            SEARCH:  Wharton, Edith, 1962-1937.
                        FIGURE 1
```

As new bibliographic records are loaded into ORION each week from the OCLC transaction tape, as new bibliographic records are keyed locally into the monographic, serial, or in-process files, or as any heading on records in these three files is edited to another form, the headings from these records are compared with headings already in the name authority file. When an incoming heading matches a heading in the file, an additional link is posted against that heading. When an incoming heading does not match a heading in the file, a new authority record is added. When an incoming heading matches a cross reference, the conflicting heading prints out on an edit list for review.

As part of the tapeloading/record creation process, an 035 field with the word "AACR2" is added to each new authority record taken from a Library of Congress bibliographic record coded in the fixed field as being cataloged following the provisions of AACR2. As catalog maintenance staff work with headings, they may add an 035 field with the word "VALID" to any heading which they judge as authoritative to use but which does not require a full authority record. The presence of the words AACR2 or VALID in the 035 field causes a plus sign to display on the browse results screen used by library staff, thus simplifying the provenance of the heading for cataloging and processing staff and allowing for specially tailored products described below. (See line R7 in Figure 1.) Figure 2 shows a sample ORION authority record.

RECORD STRUCTURE

All records in ORION are stored in alphabetical order, using a machine-generated filing prefix. In Figure 2 the filing prefix for Edith Wharton appears at the top of the record with the dates converted to lower case letters in order to arrange the filing of numbers before letters. This conversion prevents the cross reference for Wharton, Edith Newbold Jones, 1867-1937 from being filed before all the entries for Wharton, Edith, 1867-1937. The ORION authority record consists of the fixed field data displayed in the 008 field, the LC authority record number in the 010 field, the locally added 035 field, the authoritative entry in the 1XX field, see and see also references in fields 4XX and 5XX, and a number of locally defined

EXAMPLE OF ORION AUTHORITY RECORD

```
RECORD 1 OF 7
WHARTON EDITH aaaaaabigc-aaaaaabjdh  100 1
  LINK(S) TO BIBLIOGRAPHIC RECORDS (BIBLINKS):   116.
  <00> 008-0 LN/___,D/C,E/_____, ELVN,GP/_,M/_,RSD,S/R,T/N,HU/___,
NAM/A,AST/A,RFS/A,GEO/N,ROM/_,SHS/N,TYS/N,NUM/N,RUP/A,ARR/A
  <00>010-0 __$a 79151500
  <00>035-1 __$a LOCK
  <00>100-0 __$a Wharton, Edith, $d 1862-1937.
  <00>400-1 __$a Olivieri, David, $d 1862-1937.
  <00>400-2 __$a Wharton, Edith Newbold Jones, $d 1867-1937 $w nnaa
  <00>1010-0  X98,0Y18,0
  <00>1011-0  XD M24138980 (etc.)
```

FIGURE 2

fields. The 1010 field carries information about the number of works by and works about the authoritative heading. The 1011 field carries information about the location of records linked to this heading. XD indicates that the first bibliographic record linked to the heading is a work by an author whose last name begins with D and the record number 4138980 is located in file M2. The other 115 record numbers linked to the heading have been deleted from the example.

SEARCHING

The online name authority file can be accessed in two ways. Using the command "Browse Name" (bna) followed by the search term(s), one calls up in alphabetical order all the headings which match the search term(s). The second command, "List Name" (lna), followed by the search term(s) in entry order is an exact search. One enters the file either at the matching term or at the term which comes closest to matching the search term(s). From this point one can browse alphabetically backwards and forwards from the entry point in the file. Thus, one can search sequentially through the file from a particular point as in the manual card file, or one can see all the terms which match the search parameters, a particularly useful way to search when one knows the key words in the heading but is not certain of the entry element. (See Figure 3.)

The display of search results gives the total number of bibliographic records which have used each heading. From this display it

```
CURRENT SEARCH:  bna smith          CURRENT SEARCH: lna smith

R1  1  Abdy, Maria Smith.           R1  2  Smith, A.
R2  4  *Abel-Smith, Brian.          R2  2  *Smith, A. (Alwyn)
R3  5  *Abel-Smith, Patsy           R3  1  +Smith, A. C. H.  (Anthony
R4  2  Adams, Smith, 1828-                 Charles H.), 1935-

                            etc.

                        FIGURE 3
```

is possible for cataloging staff to call up the authority record, which may or may not contain cross reference information, and add, delete, or correct the heading or the associated references. This display and editing option is available to authorized cataloging staff. However, by choosing a line number from the results screen, all users of the system can see all of the bibliographic records which use that heading. In the display of each heading, works by an author file before works about the author.

AUTHORITY RECORD STATUSES

A key element of file construction is the nine record statuses which have been defined for name authority records. By assigning different statuses for different conditions, we can distinguish provisional authority headings created from in-process records from more authoritative headings created as part of the cataloging process and identify some authority problems for resolution. The statuses are:

Status 1 — all headings from the monograph and serial files

Status 2 — all headings from the in-process file

Status 3 — full authority records which have no bibliographic records linked to them

Status 4 — authority records for untraced series

Status 5 — see references generated from 4XX fields in authority records (except for untraced series)

Status 6 — see also references generated from 5XX fields in authority records (except for untraced series)

Status 7 — see references generated from 4XX fields in authority records for untraced series

Status 8 — see also references generated from 5XX fields in authority records for untraced series

Status 9 — see references from full authority records (status 1 and 3) which are coded in the $w as once valid headings no longer used under AACR2

The presence of status 3, 4, 7, 8, and 9 records is suppressed from the screen used by the public but does display on staff screens.

PRODUCTS AND CATALOG MAINTENANCE

As a result of the file structure, the record statuses, and the loading program for bibliographic records, a number of edit lists are produced which aid in quality control and which have allowed a number of procedural changes in the cataloging of items with Library of Congress AACR2 copy. To eliminate the possibility of introducing further error into the database, the computer program does not institute an automatic substitution of the authoritative heading. In all cases trained staff ascertain the nature of the problem, decide on the correct resolution, and institute the correction. In the last year catalog maintenance staff have been able to double the number of headings corrected using the global update capability of the authority module.

The highest priority in catalog maintenance is given to the list of headings from bibliographic records which conflict with see references already in the authority file when the loading program checks the headings from incoming bibliographic records against what is already in the name authority file. The records containing these headings are added to the appropriate bibliographic file but the non-valid heading cannot be added or linked in the name authority file until it has been corrected. Another edit list contains headings for traced series which match Status 4 non-traced series authority records. When typing records directly online or editing an existing bibliographic record, operators are alerted to the presence of a cross reference conflict with a heading being keyed.

It is also possible to print out a list of the new headings and the new headings from Library of Congress AACR2 records. With the latter list, which is produced monthly, we have been able to effect a major change in the way we process incoming material with Library of Congress AACR2 records. We work under three assumptions with Library of Congress AACR2 bibliographic records: (1) there should be LC authority records for all of the headings on such a bibliographic record; and (2) entries already in the ORION name authority file do not need to be checked because the necessary authority work has already been done; and (3) only the headings that are new to the name authority file need to be checked against the LC Name Authority File. Instead of checking all headings on these records prior to cataloging, only the series tracing decision is checked against our local decision. This change has contributed to a 16% increase in productivity in number of titles cataloged with LC AACR2 copy in the last fiscal year.

PROBLEMS

The authority format was one of the last MARC formats to be developed. Although there has been an effort to harmonize the coding among the various MARC bibliographic formats, the authority format was not included in this effort and some maneuvering is necessary in order to change bibliographic fields into the appropriate form used in authority records.

Filing Indicators

The non-filing indicators for the authority record are always in the first indicator position while they are in either the first or second indicator position in the bibliographic record. The Indicators column on the far right in Appendix I specifies the necessary changes for the programmer. All non-filing elements are dropped in uniform title authority records.

Series

Series to be included in the authority file are identified in a number of different ways—400, 410, 411, 440, 800, 810, 811, 830, and 840. Therefore, in constructing the file some series are coded as 130 and others as 1XX with subfields $a and $t. This does not allow for the ready identification of those which are series and those which are author/title combinations from 1XX/240, 6XX $a and $t, or 7XX $a and $t codings in the bibliographic record. Because of this ambiguity in the bibliographic records, it is problematic to use the dynamic update capability, and it is doubtful that the programming could ever be made sufficiently sensitive to recognize the different situations and respond appropriately. Also, since the authority record for the 130 field drops any non-filing characters, one would not be able to proliferate the correct text to the bibliographic record in all cases even if the programming was in place.

Uniform Titles

Uniform title entries and series titles are both coded 130 in the MARC authority format. This does not allow for machine differentiation of the two in cases in which one would like to specify programming to handle uniform titles but not series or vice versa. The possible combination of authors and uniform titles presents a particularly worrisome problem. There are four situations involving title-page titles and uniform titles which should interfile in the name authority file so that users of the file are not presented with incomplete information. The four situations are

1. Author/title-page title.

   100 10 $a Shakespeare, William, $d 1564-1616.
   245 10 $a Hamlet : $b a play / $c by William Shakespeare. . . .

2. Author/interposed uniform title.

   100 10 $a Shakespeare, William, $d 1564-1616.

240 10 $a Hamlet
245 14 $a The tragedy of Hamlet / $c by William Shakes-
      peare.

3. Author/uniform title subject.

100 10 $a Gielgud, John.
245 14 $a The staging of Shakespeare's Hamlet . . .
600 10 $a Shakespeare, William, $d 1564-1616. $t Hamlet.

4. Author/uniform title added entry.

100 10 $a Shakespeare, William, $d 1564-1616.
245 10 $a Macbeth ; $b Hamlet / $c by William Shakespeare.
700 12 $a Shakespeare, William, $d 1564-1616. $t Hamlet.

With the current name authority specifications these four records
do not display together. All four appear in the main file for Shakespeare, William, 1564-1616, but appear in different places. Numbers 1 and 2 sub-arrange under Hamlet, number 3 files under
Gielgud, and number 4 arranges under Macbeth. Also, numbers 2,
3, and 4 create a separate entry for Shakespeare, William, 1564-
1616. Hamlet., which appears after the main Shakespeare heading.

A search in the main file under Shakespeare, William will yield
only some of the library's holdings of Hamlet arranged at that point.
In order to have all editions of Hamlet one must also search the
separate Hamlet grouping after the main Shakespeare file. A search
of that latter file alone will also yield incomplete results. We have
opted for this course of action, which handles approximately 90
percent of the file correctly; however, it is the large and, it might be
argued, more important headings that are confusing and whose arrangement is difficult to explain to unsophisticated users.

There are three alternative solutions which have been considered:

1. Since only situation number 1 does not file correctly, add a
   240 field to each bibliographic record in situations 2-4. While
   240 fields are not mandated in situation number 1 in which the
   title-page title and the uniform title are the same, the cataloging rules and bibliographic utility inputting standards do not
   explicitly prohibit adding a uniform title in these cases. However, this solution requires an extraordinary amount of human

intervention and may still result in the display of some of an author's works with a separate entry and some in the unsubdivided file.

2. Ignore the uniform titles in situations 2-4 so that no separate files will be created. The result of this action would be that the only separate authority headings for authors would be for subject subdivisions, such as — Biography or — Bibliography. All of an author's works would arrange under his name without further subdivision. This solution is appealing because it is the same arrangement used in the card catalog, which would make for an easy transition from one to the other. However, if it is decided to accept this method, a meaningful arrangement must be made within the unsubdivided author heading. Given the current organization of the name authority file, there is no place within the second level of hierarchy to store the authority records for author/uniform title headings and to create and display the cross references generated from these records.

3. Another solution is the complete opposite of the above. Instead of providing no access under title, change the program to create an author/title entry for each 1XX/245 combination and interfile them with the records for the author/uniform title entries currently being created. The result of this action would be that there would be no files for the author unsubdivided. Instead the resulting authority file would be gigantic and therefore difficult to use by many library patrons.

CONCLUSIONS

Although the MARC format does not allow for a completely satisfactory conversion of bibliographic headings to authority headings, the usability of the resulting online name authority file by library staff and the public has not been seriously affected. The ORION online authority control module provides for better and more consistent access for all users than its manual counterparts. Its establishment has streamlined online maintenance procedures and has led to a number of procedural changes in the cataloging with copy process with a resulting increase in productivity.

NOTES

1. For a full history and technical description of UCLA's ORION system, James Fayollat and Elizabeth Coles, "Database Management Principles of the UCLA Library's ORION System," *Information Technology and Libraries*, 6, no. 2 (June 1987): 102-15.

2. Over the last three years the UCLA Library has been engaged in several large retrospective conversion projects, which have added over a million older bibliographic records to ORION. A substantial portion of the money has been assigned to authority cleanup, but this process is being carried out after conversion working from edit lists from ORION. Consequently, at the present time the online authority files sometimes contain multiple entries for the same entity.

APPENDIX I

ORION NAME AUTHORITY FILE SPECIFICATIONS

TYPE	AU TAG	BY/ ABOUT	BIB FIELD AND TAG	SUBFIELDS	INDICATORS
Personal Name	100				
		x	MC/TC 100	a,q,b,c,d,k,l, m,o,r,s	For all MC/TC 100, 400, 600, 692, 700, 800 - 1st from bib field; set 2nd to 0
		x	IP 100	a	For all IP 100, 600, 700--Set 1st to 1; set 2nd to 0
		x	MC/TC 400	a,q,b,c,d,t,n,p, k,l,m,o,r,s	
		x	IP 400	a	IP records with indicators; keep indicators from bib. field
		y	MC/TC 600	a,q,b,c,d,t,n,p, k,l,m,o,r,s,x,y,z	
		y	IP 600	a	
		y	TC 692	a,q,b,c,d,t,n,p, k,l,m,o,r,s,x,y,z	
		x	MC/TC 700	a,q,b,c,d,t,n,p k,l,m,o,r,s	

APPENDIX I (continued)

TYPE	AU TAG	BY/ ABOUT	BIB FIELD AND TAG		SUBFIELDS	INDICATORS
		x	IP	700	a	
		x	MC/TC	800	a,q,b,c,d,t,n,p, k,l,m,o,r,s	
Corporate Name	110					
		x	MC/TC	110	a,b,n,d,c,k,g, l,m,o,r,s	For all MC/TC 110, 410, 610, 693, 710, 810-- 1st from bib. field; set 2nd to 0
		x	IP	110	a	For all IP 110, 610, 710--Set 1st to 2; set 2nd to 0
		x	MC/TC	410	a,b,n,d,c,k,g, l,m,o,r,s	
		x	IP	410	a (up to space before semicolon; drop 1st and last characters in field if they are parentheses)	
		y	MC/TC	610	a,b,n,d,c,k,g, l,m,o,r,s,t,p, x,y,z	
		y	IP	610	a	
		y	TC	693	a,b,n,d,c,k,g, l,m,o,r,s,t,p, x,y,z	
		x	MC/TC	710	a,b,n,d,c,k,g, l,m,o,r,s,t,p	
		x	IP	710	a	
		x	MC/TC	810	a,b,n,d,c,k,g, l,m,o,r,s,t,p	
Conference Name	111					
		x	MC/TC	111	a,q,b,n,d,c,e, g,k,l	For all MC/TC 111 411, 611, 694, 711, 811--1st from bib field; set 2nd to 0

APPENDIX I (continued)

TYPE	AU TAG	BY/ ABOUT	BIB FIELD AND TAG		SUBFIELDS	INDICATORS
		x	IP	111	a	For all IP 111, 611, 711--Set 1st to 2; set 2nd to 0
		x	MC/TC	411	a,q,b,n,d,c,e, g,k,l,t,p	
		x	IP	411	a (up to space before semicolon; drop 1st and last characters in field if they are parentheses)	
		y	MC/TC	611	a,q,b,n,d,c,e, g,k,l,t,p,x,y,z	
		y	IP	611	a	
		y	TC	694	a,q,b,n,d,c,e, g,k,l,t,p,x,y,z	
		x	MC/TC	711	a,q,b,n,d,c,e, g,k,l,t,p	
		x	IP	711	a	
		x	MC/TC	811	a,q,b,n,d,c,e, g,k,l,t,p	
Series/ Uniform Title	130	x	MC/TC	130	a,n,p,l,f,k,m, o,r,s,g,d	For all MC/TC/IP 130, 400, 440, 630, 695, 730, 830, 840--Set 1st to (underscore); set 2nd to 0
		x	IP	130	a	
		x	IP	400	a (up to space before semicolon; drop 1st and last characters in field if they are parentheses)	
		x	MC/TC	440	a,n,p,l	
		x	IP	440	a (up to space before semicolon; drop 1st and last characters in field if they are parentheses)	

APPENDIX I (continued)

TYPE	AU TAG	BY/ ABOUT	BIB FIELD AND TAG	SUBFIELDS	INDICATORS
		y	MC/TC 630	a,n,p,x,y,z,d,l,m, o,r,s	
		y	TC 695	a,n,p,l,d,m,o,r,s, x,y,z	
		x	MC/TC 730	a,n,p,l,f,k,m, o,r,s,g,d	
		x	MC/TC 830	a,n,p,l	
		x	MC/TC 840	a,n,p,l	
Uniform Title	100,110 111	x	MC/TC 1xx/240		Drop subfields f, h in 240
		x	IP 1xx/240		No indicators

Uniform title instructions: Check the 240 1st indicator. If it is
0, ignore the 240 field. If it is 1, check for the presence of a
1xx field. If there is not a 1xx field, ignore the 240. If
there is a 1xx field, select it and follow the appropriate 1xx
rule above for indicators and subfields to be selected. Drop the
number of leading characters as indicated by the 240 2nd
indicator and place the data from the 240 field at the end of the
data for the 1xx, and before the field tag, record status and
indicators selected for the matching prefix. Change the 240 $a
to $t; leave the other subfields tagged as is. If an authority
record is generated, the data from the 240 field will be the $t
of the 1xx field.